LOOK AFTER THE PENNIES

100s OF MONEY-SAVING TIPS AND TRICKS

TESS READ

Michael O'Mara Books Limited

First published in Great Britain in 2011 by
Michael O'Mara Books Limited
9 Lion Yard
Tremadoc Road
London SW4 7NQ

A CIP catalogue record for this book is available from the British Library.

Papers used by Michael O'Mara Books Limited are natural, recyclable products made from wood grown in sustainable forests. The manufacturing processes conform to the environmental regulations of the country of origin.

ISBN: 978-1-84317-610-7 in paperback print format
ISBN: 978-1-84317-775-3 in EPub format
ISBN: 978-1-84317-776-0 in Mobipocket format

1 2 3 4 5 6 7 8 9 10

Cover design by Burville-Riley Partnership

Designed and typeset by K.DESIGN, Winscombe, Somerset

Printed and bound in Great Britain by Cox and Wyman

www.mombooks.com

LOOK AFTER THE PENNIES

Tess Read is a freelance writer and a former employee of the Bank of England. The author of several books, her work has been published in the *Financial Times* and *Euromoney*, among other publications, and she has completed courses in macro- and microeconomics at the London School of Economics. Her long-suffering husband and children agree that if only she would trade in writing books for a more profitable career, she could count the pounds rather than look after the pennies. But she is too busy counting her pennies to listen.

TO ROSIE

For all the savings we have to make to afford you.
But you're worth it.

ACKNOWLEDGEMENTS

Huge massive enormous hugs and thanks and kisses to Glendra, my mum, not only for her devoted support, but also for her wisdom about old-fashioned ways to save money on everything and anything. Thanks also to Danny, as ever, although unusually he didn't write any of this book.

Thanks also for all the tips and hints and collective wisdom from friends and relatives near and far – GG, Roo, Dad, Denise, Gisèle, Amy, Natasha, Delli, Behnoush, Calum, Amy, Sam, Darren, Graham, Nick, Maria-Jose, Maria, Ben, Milly, Tijen, Claire, Elena, Fliff, Ian, Veronica, Cushla, Alan, Lisa, Anna, April, Sarah T, Sarah N, Tom, Andy and David. And a thank you to all those kind, supportive people who help me along in other important ways: Anne, Audrey, Chrissie, Lesley, Hilary, Vilma, Celie, Alice, Tom, Alex and Annie.

Thanks also to Kate and Katie, my lovely publishers. And Joe and Poppy – the future generation – for giving me reasons to save.

Tess Read

Contents

1. Introduction

We are working harder and living longer than previous generations so there is more reason than ever to save money and to make sure that we are living better. The advent of the Internet is giving us, the consumers, more and more opportunities to compare prices and get together to pool resources, and so beat the retailers at their own game. And as worldwide consumption is hugely on the increase, it makes sense to sit back and reflect on what we can actually afford, what we actually need, and which choices are best for the earth and for all of our futures.

Look After the Pennies will help you to:

👍 Save while you shop, without having to buy economy mince

👍 Plan a monthly budget, without any cries of desperation or panic

👍 Create lovely presents for a fraction of shop prices

And hopes to bring cheer to your heart with hundreds of ideas for how to save thousands of pounds, not to mention teaching you how to clean your home with a lemon (yes, really).

But first, the **three golden rules** for living well in the modern age:

1. MORE EXPENSIVE IS NOT NECESSARILY BETTER

The DVD player for £100 is not necessarily better made nor will produce a better picture than the one for £50. The same is certainly true of a T-shirt or a dress, especially if the cheaper one actually suits you better.

2. BUY THINGS ONLY BECAUSE YOU NEED OR LOVE THEM

Temptation is everywhere, more and more so with increased branding, sponsorship and even embedded adverts streamed onto your mobile while you're minding your own business. Always try to be conscious of what you actually need and will really value, not what a shop or someone on a Facebook page wants to sell you.

3. MANAGE YOUR MONEY

Don't let it rule you – know how much you have, or don't have, and plan accordingly. We know your bank manager is unlikely to be your best friend, but neither is your bank account. If you have a regular wage your salary will appear in it as a nice lump sum, but all the utilities and direct debits have to come off that before you can even think about what might be left over. Put yourself in charge of those pounds, as well as all the pennies that go with them.

Before you start

A lot of the ideas in this book need access to the Internet to bring them to life. If you don't have access then your first port of call is your local library, which will provide free Internet access, and you don't even have to join the library (although if you do join you can borrow books for free too). If you are using library Internet access, it makes sense to make a list before you go of all the things you would like to research or compare prices on.

Pool your resources

To save money every day in the world that we live in, we should all pool our resources and **reduce, re-use, freecycle, borrow, lend and share**. Here is a flavour of just some of the ideas that I talk about in this book for how we can all help each other to save money:

👍 Go swapping instead of shopping

👍 Get connected with other people to borrow a car or tent or gazebo, rather than buy one

👍 Rent out your bicycle or hedge trimmer or Xbox for the day

👍 Club together to swap restaurant vouchers

👍 Use the Internet to find items other people no longer need, and give away what you don't need any more to charity or to somebody else who could still make use of it

👍 Park your car for a few £s in someone's drive, rather than for a fortune in an NCP

Exchange those shopping trips for a weekend away in a borrowed caravan, or have a hairdresser cut your hair and in return you wash their car. If we share the wealth then there's more to go round.

Save all those pennies and we're helping to save the planet too. If we turn away from the retailers' plan to make us always desire the new, we can spend less, buy less, but have more.

2. Shopping: Make Technology Work for You

GET ONLINE

Freecycle

It's big and it's brilliant. Freecycle is a way of finding something you have been looking for, which somebody else might be happy to give away to you, for free, and finding people to give away your unwanted things to. You can find everything on freecycle – tents, bikes, maps, shoes, watches, furniture. You name it, it's there.

There are more than 500 freecycle networks in the UK and hundreds more around the world – check out if there is one near you at **uk.freecycle.org**, also look at the other similar sites **ilovefreegle.org** and **freegive.co.uk**. They are all simple to use – just sign up and you can opt to receive emails alerting you to when new items have become available or to items that people want to get hold of.

If there isn't already a freecycle network in your area, set one up.

Swapping not shopping

Don't go shopping when you could go swapping – check out **swapz.co.uk** or **swapshop.co.uk** to find out about the hundreds of things you could swap with hundreds of people. Check out swishing (see page 25) for clothes swaps.

Hiring not buying

Many of the things we want or need are for a limited period or for a particular event. For example, if you want a tent to camp for a week in the summer, you don't really need it cluttering up your house for the rest of the year – look to **ecomodo.com**: a peer-to-peer site that lets you hire from a stranger at a fraction of the cost of buying new.

Through ecomodo you can hire anything from a bicycle pump to a paper guillotine, an evening dress to an airbed or even an Xbox. You can see what is on offer near you or where you might be going, and you can sign up to see updates of what becomes available in your area. Join the circle, make a little money on the things that you have to loan out, and cut the shops clean out of the profit.

Shared ownership

If six of us each buy a sixth of something, then between us we have the whole thing. Shared ownership is a new concept in shopping – you can share the ownership of anything from a classic car to a work of art. There are sites that link people who are interested in potential ownership of an expensive product but can't afford to buy one outright. Together you can own something that you can each use.

Check out **fractionallife.com** *to find out what the possibilities are for you.*

Transition towns

These are locally formed community groups, which have some very practical outcomes, e.g.:

👍 Starting a car-sharing scheme

👍 Creating a shared 'tool library'

👍 Matching green-fingered people without gardens with garden owners who only have regular coloured fingers

Joining a transition town can get you access to:

👍 Fresh apples for free from a community orchard

👍 A loaned power drill for some weekend DIY

👍 People willing to help you put up those shelves in return for you helping them out when they come to paint their kitchen

Transition towns are formed to be practical local initiatives against climate change – check out **localpower.org.uk** to find out if there is a transition town near you, and look at **transitionnetwork.org** to see other things they do, for example garden sharing.

Community action

Taking transition towns a step further, there are sites which encourage and facilitate people to get involved in community action micro projects to help us in our saving money and living-well ways – e.g. if you want to get more cycle lanes put into your local area the first rung on the ladder is for someone to map the existing cycle lanes. This concept is still quite American driven, e.g. check out **IfWeRanTheWorld.com**, but the movement is growing in the UK too.

LETS

Local exchange trading schemes (LETS) are friendly local skill-swapping schemes where you offer what you can do, e.g. helping to paint a house, washing a car, cutting hair or removing rubbish, and you can 'bank' the thank yous you receive in order to trade them later for whatever it is *you* need – restaurant meals, someone to fix your computer etc. The concept of LETS barter systems is of course as old as the hills, but the use of the Internet takes them to a new level – it is now so easy to connect with other peoples' needs and for them to find out yours.

Check out **lets-linkup.com** *or* **letslink.org.uk** *to find if there is a LETS in your area, or somewhere you plan to travel to. Set one up if there isn't – your bank balance will love you for it.*

If you don't have a LETS near you and don't fancy setting one up, fairs at local schools often have 'auctions of promises' where you bid money which goes to the school in return for someone's time and skill, e.g. I recently had a fabulous reflexology treatment this way for less than its usual cost and the money went to help the school.

Mobile Internet

The rules of the game for shopping have changed dramatically since the advent of the Internet. If you have mobile Internet and can check comparative prices of goods in one shop while you are in another – you can bargain with almost everybody. Point out to one shop that another is selling the same product for a cheaper price and the shop you are in is quite likely to drop its price to match. Use technology well and you can save £££s.

Using shop bots

Shop bots are automatic tools that search thousands of websites for their prices on a given product you are searching for, e.g. **kelkoo.co.uk**, **megashopbot.com**. These are fantastic tools for finding the cheapest price for identical, or near identical, products. **Moneysavingexpert.com** has devised a shop bot that searches through the shop bots and aims to give you the most comprehensive picture, and this is certainly useful to look at when shopping around.

Shop bots on the move

Often the most useful time to access a shop bot is when you are out shopping and see a product you like, but wonder if the price being offered really *is* the most competitive. If your phone can access the web, try **kelkoo.co.uk**, which has a mobile-friendly version of its site. **Shopsavvy.com** has an app designed for Google Android phones, while **twenga.com** has developed an app for iPhones – or just look for prices on Google or Amazon.

Beware possible charges for accessing the Internet on your phone – in most cases it is free or only a few pence for such a search, but do check your phone deal. You don't want the search costs to outweigh the saving on the product.

Is cashback for real?

Yes it is. There are a bunch of websites which give you money back on your purchase (cashback) if you buy products through them. The reason they do this is because they receive a payment from the retailer from whom you are buying and they kick back some or all of this payment to you. (In case you are wondering how they can still make money this way, it is from the adverts on their site.) The big cashback sites also negotiate some exclusive deals with retailers. This means you can buy things you frequently buy from regular shops, e.g. M&S, Halfords etc., and you receive a percentage of cashback, typically 5%, on your purchase.

Pitfalls of cashback

It can definitely be worth buying through cashback sites but make sure that you never pay to register with any. When buying through a cashback site be sure that you click to purchase straight from the cashback site – if you go a roundabout route you might not get paid.

Indeed, you should also be prepared when using cashback sites for sometimes not getting paid when you expected to – sometimes the cashback site may not have been paid by the retailer for unexpected reasons, and if so, you won't get your kickback either. The industry is not highly regulated so if you don't receive cashback, you have few rights to demand it. Don't focus on the cashback at the expense of getting the best price for the product.

> *Be sure you draw the money out of the cashback's account and into your own bank account as soon as possible, because you can't count it as yours until it really is.*

Best cashback sites

👍 **Topcashback.co.uk**, **cashbacknetwork.co.uk**, and **giveortake.com** kick back to you 100% cashback (i.e. all the payment they receive from the retailer) and all charge no annual fee

👍 **Quidco.com** kicks back to you the full amount it receives from the retailer but charges a £5 annual fee

👍 There are many other cashback sites, e.g. **freefivers.co.uk**, that could offer the best cashback for a particular shop even though they don't pass on 100% of the cashback they receive

👍 **Moneysavingexpert.com** has a tool you can use to search for the best cashback on any given shop

> *Be wary of using too many cashback sites because you don't get the money back from any of them until you've reached a certain level of cashback, so it doesn't pay to spread it around.*

Cashback for charity

Rather than keeping all your cashback money you could choose to give some away to a charity of your choice – **cashbacknetwork.co.uk** has an option whereby you can donate a portion of your cashback earnings to charity, and the website **thegivingmachine.co.uk** is an organization which arranges cashback for you and then donates it all to a charity or school of your choice.

Cashback when out and about

If you register your credit or debit card with **quidco.com** they will make a note of any payments you make on the high street and you will earn cashback from them. This means that you can earn cashback from your regular high street purchases as well as online. Currently, this option is only available for a few shops, but quidco may expand their range.

Credit card cashback

There is an even simpler way to earn cashback when you shop and that's by using a cashback credit card. See the Credit Cards and Debt Management chapter for the best credit card cashback deals.

Voucher fun

You can get great deals with money-off vouchers for all sorts of things:

 Groupon.com is the biggest voucher site – you put in your location and it tells you what deals are near you, also sending you an email a day with the best local deals

👍 **Vouchercodes.co.uk** is another big site which boasts many exclusive deals with retailers and an easy search facility

👍 Vouchercloud is an app for your phone which lets you narrow down the possible deals by type or radius from you, or purely alphabetically

The sites **myvouchercodes.co.uk** and **hotukdeals.com** are interactive so that the most popular deals are put to the top of the list. However, like most voucher sites, they are very busy sites which can make searching for the deal you are after difficult, and in the meantime encourage you to be tempted by a deal you don't need. Although you can get some great offers by signing up to voucher sites, sign up to too many and you can be tempted too often – it can be a good idea to unsubscribe to emails regularly and then subscribe again when you are planning a shopping trip.

Other voucher sites to try are **freestuff.co.uk**, **magicfreebiesuk.co.uk**, **voucherfreebies.co.uk**, **freebiesiteuk.co.uk** and **freebieheaven.co.uk**.

SUMMARY

From price comparison shopping 'bots' to cashback deals and vouchers, there are many fabulous innovations which can really help you save £££s whether you shop online or on the high street. But don't let the era of deals and discounts tempt you into more consumption than you actually need – a saving isn't a saving if you don't need or even really want the thing you buy. Thrift comes too late when you find it at the bottom of your purse, as someone once said.

3. Shopping: When and Where to Shop

HANDY HINTS FOR THE MODERN SHOPPER

Think counter cyclical

👍 Buy your Christmas cards/expensive crackers for next year at half price in January

👍 Stock a 'present drawer' with goodies from the January sales

👍 Buy your clothes for next summer in the August and September sell-off sales, and your next year's winter gloves and coat in the January sales

Shop cheap

Shop in cheap areas of town, even if you're lucky enough to be living in an expensive area. Prices in all sorts of shops vary by area – from cobblers to chain shops. Shops in cheaper locations will often have more promotions on. But beware corner shops as these always charge higher prices than larger shops.

Always try *bargaining*

It's surprising how much difference the offer of cash and a smile can make to a price in a shop, even a chain shop. Independent shops will often give you a discount, but you have to ask for one. Good lines to use are 'Can you do something on the price for this please?' or 'If I buy two will you give me a discount?' Small chain shops will often bargain when their sale is on, and even major high street names will bargain if you're buying something expensive from them – a friend when buying his work suits always asks for an extra 20% off the sale price, and usually gets at least a 10% reduction.

Know the rule of three

If you're in a shop where the prices are set by the person in front of you (where the goods have no prices on them and you have to ask), and the prices bear a nebulous relation to the cost of the item – i.e. where bargaining is the name of the game, such as in an antique shop – you need to know the rules:

1. As you walk round the shop don't look too interested in or excited by anything in particular.
2. Ask the price of three items in turn; you aren't interested in the first two items but the third one is the one you actually want. Now you've got a decent first price to work with, but still bargain from this.
3. Look a little displeased, giving you time to do some quick mental maths to take off another 15%, and suggest that price. You should end up with a price somewhere between their price and your discounted offer.

Tips for buying and selling on eBay

EBay is the world's biggest auction website where you can either bid for items or agree with the seller on a 'buy it now' price. (Make sure to look only at **ebay.co.uk** so you don't end up buying something from Zanzibar by mistake.) You can get particularly good bargains for children's items as little ones are always growing and families need to move things on. And although eBay is a re-sale site, many items are new and boxed, and by shopping around you can significantly undercut the high street.

👍 Look for items that are listed Collection In Person Only. They always sell for less, and even if you can't collect in person you'll usually find that the seller is happy to have it picked up by a courier, which could still save you money on the price

👍 Decide your maximum price for something you bid for, put it into your settings when you make a bid and stick to it

👍 Look beyond the obvious category for an item – there are usually two or three other categories that will overlap, and sometimes sellers list things in these instead. Because the items are then harder to find, they can sell for less

👍 Sometimes sellers list items with a Buy It Now price that is much lower than the true value. There are real bargains to be had this way but you'll need to put a lot of time into looking and be very, very quick on the draw

👍 For selling, if you are brave enough to do it, a reserve price of 99p will often end up going for the highest end price, and incurs the lowest fees

Auctions

You can get great bargains from auctions – wooden furniture such as tables are particularly good value as they can sell for very little, and it's easy to tell if they are structurally sound or not. Electrical items are much trickier to assess, i.e. how long they will last, and so they are best avoided. Time was you often had to pay for a catalogue but now you can usually download them for free. Make sure you decide the price you are prepared to pay and stick to it – don't be tempted into a bidding war. You can bid online without needing to go to the auction but you do lose information about the products by not being able to see them.

> *For lists of auctions, what they are selling and online bidding look at* **ukauctioneers.com,** *and* **ukauctionguides.co.uk.**

Clothes shopping

Always buy what suits you best, rather than the latest fashion. It will last you longer and you'll get more wear out of your clothes.

Treat your wardrobe as if it was a shop

Which of the clothes in your wardrobe would you actually buy today? If you wouldn't want to buy it from a shop, then don't keep it in your house. You can give old clothes to charity or sell them, e.g. on eBay. Selling a job lot is a good idea if you can't face the hassle of many individual sales.

Buying from charity shops

Make sure the clothes fit you or that you can alter them – it's easy to be beguiled by price or style into buying something that would work for you if only it were in another size. But it isn't. When buying from charity shops try to ignore price and really look at the clothes you are picking up to see whether you actually like them and whether they would be useful to you.

Beware shoes from charity shops – if they have been worn at all they will have been worn down in ways that don't match your feet and could well cause blisters.

Clothes swaps – swishing

Swishing parties are a great fun way of getting new clothes without any expense, and with a good deal of fun. Get together with a group of friends and each brings their unwanted clothes, preferably in anonymous black bags which are all emptied together on to a big table or the floor (to prevent embarrassment). Sort through, try on, have a laugh, keep the good ones, and give the rest to charity.

You don't even need friends to swap with – check out **swishing.com** to see if someone has already organized a swishing party near you. You bring along an unwanted outfit or two, buy a ticket for entry (around £3 and the money goes to charity), and then you can take home whatever you want or need. As the founder of swishing says, swishing parties are for people who 'want to combine glamour, environmental protection, and frugality'. Sounds like you? Then get swishing.

Designer clothes at a fraction of the price

There are lots of Internet sites offering designer clothes cut price:

 Get The Label, **getthelabel.com**, where you can get Jack Jones or Police for men and Rare, French Connection or Iska for women for about half price

👍 Fashionista Outlet, **fashionista-outlet.com**, offer some designer labels at 60% off such as Roberto Cavalli, Versace and Alexander McQueen

👍 Brand Alley, **brandalley.co.uk**, take up to 70% off top names in fashion such as Ted Baker, Cath Kidston, Gucci and Armani

👍 T.K. Maxx has online and high street presence and is great for men, women and children's clothes, but you have to put the time in and hunt around for your bargains

Charity shops can have designer bargains – look at the charity shops in expensive areas or near major transport hubs, e.g. the British Red Cross near Victoria station in London always has expensive labels such as men's Hugo Boss or Crombie and Reiss suits for very low prices.

Outlet villages

Check out **shopping-villages.co.uk** for a searchable database of all the shopping outlet villages and factory outlet shops in the UK. You can get great bargains at these shops with high-end products selling for far less than their high street price, but make sure you need what you buy!

There are many websites offering discounts at shopping villages but these are rarely worth it – you have to pay to join their scheme so to feel that you are getting value for money you have to keep spending.

Vintage

Most towns have one or two vintage clothes shops which often do good priced, unusual clothing, or you can get vintage online through Oxfam, **oxfam.org.uk/vintage**.

SUMMARY

Planning ahead and shopping in different areas of town can land you with some brilliant bargains. And the Internet also gives us so many ways to shop around to find the best deals, helps us to compare prices so that we can haggle, and can be used to spread the word so that we can go swapping rather than shopping. Cut out the retailer altogether and make your bank account smile. After all, it's got the monthly bills to contend with ...

4. Monthly Utility Bills

MAKE BIG SAVINGS ON YOUR MONTHLY OUTGOINGS

Get active

Take a day a year, preferably early in January, when there are special deals on offer to tempt those short on money after Christmas, to manage your utilities. Check out the competitor deals to your own, and switch if they are better.

Switching gas and electricity providers

Don't switch direct but go through a switching website and you can get cashback just for switching. Check out the offers available on **Simplyswitch.com**, **moneysupermarket.com**, **uswitch.com** and the **energyhelpline.com**. You could get £40 cashback for a switch. Switching should be straightforward as you just give the company your meter readings and they will handle all the rest. Your service will not be cut at any time or affected in any way, and they won't even need to come to your house for you to switch providers.

Cheaper energy in rural areas

If you live in a rural area with an oil-fired heater, get together with neighbours in order to create a bulk order to get a cheaper per unit price. Also be sure to buy your oil in the summer rather than the winter when the price usually goes up by at least 10%.

Dual fuel deals usually work out cheaper, but not always, so do compare with the switching websites, and bear in mind that you get half the cashback amount if you switch to one provider for both fuels, rather than to two different providers.

Take meter readings

Take meter readings regularly, e.g. once a quarter, and tell your providers the reading. They will then bill you accurately. Otherwise they can underestimate and when they finally get round to taking a reading, you will be landed with a large bill; or they can overestimate, which means they've got some of your money that could be earning interest for you.

USE LESS ENERGY

Switch off to save

Some electricity providers will give you a free energy monitor to check how much energy you use at different times. If they don't, you can buy one for around £20, e.g. from Amazon. Then see how much you can save by switching off appliances at night. Personalize your meter with the tariffs you are being charged to see precisely how much you save with different usage habits. You'll be surprised to see how much you can save by just turning lights off when you are out of a room.

Unplug electrical appliances rather than switching them off or leaving them on standby – most devices use up almost as much electricity in standby mode as when operational, and still use some electricity even when they are actually switched off but still plugged in. So unplug chargers, laptops, set top boxes, TVs etc. to make sure you aren't burning power for nothing.

Get a TV power down – this is a great device that turns off the power to your TV and to the units connected to it (e.g. set top box) when you switch off the TV with the remote control. Energy companies usually do a special deal on them, e.g. **eon-uk.com** will post you one for £3 only (to cover delivery costs). Check for special deals on **switchgasandelectric.com**.

> **Energysavingtrust.org.uk** *has a carbon cutter tool to help you calculate how much electricity, and so carbon, you use.*

Useful tips for energy saving

- 👍 Use energy-saving lightbulbs – they last up to ten times longer than ordinary bulbs and they can save you around £45 over the lifetime of the bulb. This saving can go up to £70 over the bulb's lifetime if you are replacing a high-wattage incandescent bulb, or a bulb that's used for several hours a day

- 👍 Put the temperature on the thermostat down one degree – this typically saves £50 p.a. and about 50kg in carbon emissions

👍 Check if your water is set to heat up too high – the temperature on your water cylinder should be at 60°C/140°F. You can usually find the thermostat on the boiler. You can also control the temperature on your radiators so they don't all blast out the same heat

👍 Fill up washing appliances – dishwasher, washing machine, tumble dryer. They use less electricity and less water with one full load than two half loads

👍 Use pot pourri instead of plug-in air fresheners

👍 On cold days when you have finished cooking, leave the oven door open to help heat the kitchen, as long as there aren't children around

Generate your own power, and be paid for it

If you install solar panels or a wind turbine and contribute to the national grid of energy, you can benefit from the government's 'feed-in tariff' scheme – i.e. you feed into the grid and the government pays you for your energy, even if you use it all yourself. Check out the Energy Saving Trust, **energysavingtrust.org.uk**, to find what you might make.

A rough estimate calculates that you could have 40–50% of your energy needs paid for each year, saving £££s, plus you could make £800 a year, and the cost of the initial investment would be paid back in ten to fifteen years.

The initial outlay on these products is expensive – solar panels will cost around £8,000 to £15,000 (depending on house size), and a wind turbine upwards of £25,000. The government has said a feed-in tariff will exist for at least twenty-five years, and the solar panels should last at least that long.

Tesco (yes, really) do very good value solar panels, starting from £7,000 including installation and you can get double clubcard points (13,500 of them) during promotions; also look at **southernsolar.co.uk** in the south of England, and **sandersonsolar.co.uk** and **localsolarpanelquotes.co.uk** nationwide. If you have some technical know-how, and a bit of chutzpah, the very cheapest way to get solar panels is to install them yourself, see **midsummerenergy.co.uk** for kits and for peel and stick-on solar panels on such places as caravan roofs.

Solar power to heat your water

Solar power is good at creating energy for electricity, even in the UK, but it's super-efficient at just heating water with a solar hot-water system. These systems are called solar thermal panels and they cost less to install than solar panels used for creating electricity (solar thermal panels cost around £5,000). You can expect them to provide one third of your yearly hot water needs, cutting your water heating bill by nearly £100 a year. For an explanation of the system see **britishgas.co.uk** and search for solar thermal panels. Solar thermal panels only work if you have a cistern for your hot water, not if you have a combi boiler.

Solar panels for free

An alternative to paying for solar panels is to have them installed entirely for free – you then get to use the energy they create, or the hot water they heat, but the installation company gets the money the government kicks back with the 'feed-in tariff'. So, the company makes the money back from the installation with the ongoing payments from the government for generating the electricity. But you get solar panels for free and solar energy for free, and the companies install and maintain the solar panels and all accompanying equipment for free.

There are several companies which provide this service, such as **isis-solar.com**, **ashadegreener.co.uk**, and **homesun.com** – this last website also lets you check instantly whether your roof is eligible.

Another company, **evoenergy.co.uk**, mixes the two business models – you and the company share the cost of installation, and then you share the rewards from the government pay-outs. A good compromise between upfront investment and long-term benefit.

Gadgets that pay you back

The ecobutton from Utterlyeco is a brilliant device that puts your computer into the most efficient energy-saving mode without it noticing, so that you can instantly return your computer to where you were before with no need for a restart. This means you can save electricity every time you walk away from the computer for a minute or to take a phone call.

Tangogroup.net are always evolving fabulous alternative energy-saving products, such as the shower-powered radio. This is easy to fit to most standard showers and means that you have radio waves in the shower powered just by the flow of water, with none of the corroding batteries that afflict all the millions of shower radios sold and then land-filled in Britain each year.

Small solar-powered and wind-up radios, calculators, torches and MP3 players are very cheap and durable, perfect for travelling. Try camping shops for the cheapest on the market, and **tangogroup.net** for the latest new technologies. You can also buy solar-powered and wind-up chargers for almost any electrical device, including your phone. These will save you money on batteries and they will enable you to use electrical devices anywhere out and about. (You don't need full sun for solar panels to work, just light.)

Switch to online billing

Many utility companies offer a discount for online billing, check if yours does and if so, switch to it. If you want the amount written down in paper form then find a pen and paper and jot the amount down when the email comes through. You also get a more efficient record this way rather than having sheets of paper to sift through and store.

WATER SAVINGS

Switch to a water meter?

If you live in England or Wales you can get a water meter fitted free of charge by your water company (in Scotland you have to pay for a meter). A meter can save you money if you use less water than the average for the size of property you live in.

The rule of thumb is that if there are fewer people in your house than bedrooms then you will probably save money by having a water meter. If you live alone in a multi-bedroom house you will save hundreds every year.

Find out if you are likely to save money or not with the calculators on the websites of the Consumer Council for Water and **uswitch.com**. Once you've worked out how much water your household usually uses then ask your water company how much that usage would cost and check that you would definitely make savings. Be aware that different water companies charge different amounts – but unfortunately you can't switch companies.

Read that meter

If you do have a water meter, make sure you send meter readings in, just as for the electricity and gas, to make sure you are being charged only for what you actually use.

Check your tariff

Water companies are trialling new tariffs all the time, e.g. for low water usage, or for people on benefits with three or more children. Check out what your water company is offering, and check what is upcoming on the regulator's website, **ofwat.gov.uk**.

Use less water with free gadgets

There are lots of devices that reduce your water use, which your water company will send to you for free. Check out **savewatersavemoney.com** and look for what your water company will give you for free. These include:

- Save-a-flush or water hippos, which sit inside your toilet cistern and mean you use one litre less water each time the loo is flushed. If you have a new loo installed, choose a dual flush so you can opt for short or long flush

- A 'shower save' device which prevents excess water flowing through your shower but keeps the pressure strong. You can save even more water, and water heating costs, from your shower by purchasing a clever flow compensating shower head – which uses less water but keeps pressure just as strong – from around £50 from, e.g., **ecocamel.com**. The shower head will on average pay for itself in less than a year, even if you don't have a water meter

- Tap inserts, which mix air into the water to give the illusion of the same volume of water from the tap, but actually use less

- Gel for hanging baskets in the garden to help the soil retain more water

Fix dripping taps

A dripping tap can waste 5,000 litres of water a year. Check out **leakingtaps.co.uk** for great advice on how to fix it.

Use shorter wash cycles

Try switching your regular wash on the dishwasher and washing machine to a shorter, lower temperature one and see if you can actually tell the difference. If not, stick with it and you will save water and energy, money and carbon.

Switch the tap off when you brush your teeth

A bathroom tap pours out six litres of water a minute – that's twelve litres wasted per teeth-brushing session. If everyone in the UK didn't run the tap when they brushed their teeth, we would save 446 million litres of water per year. (That's assuming nobody currently switches off the tap of course! And I know I do.)

Buy water-efficient appliances

Dishwashers and washing machines vary hugely in how much water and energy they use and some use much less energy than others, but much more water, so what you gain on the swings you lose on the roundabouts. **Comet.co.uk** lets you choose dishwashers by the litres they use per wash as well as how energy efficient they are (A-rated appliances are the most energy efficient but you should check water use too) – there are full-sized dishwashers which use as little as ten litres per cycle, but most use a third more than this, and some use almost double.

Waterwise.org.uk *awards machines the Waterwise marque for water efficiency, so check their website for advice on water-efficient products.*

No butts

Just an if. If you can get a free wheelie bin from your local council, you can convert it into a water butt to collect the 85,000 litres of rain which falls on your roof every year. You can buy a kit from **doctorenergy.co.uk**, or if you're handy you can do it yourself by fixing a tap to the bottom of the wheelie bin and making a hole in the lid for a length of hose, the other end of which you join with a water diverter to the guttering.

Otherwise you could always buy a water butt – **waterbuttsdirect.co.uk** do the cheapest ones, less than £20 a butt.

Cut the crap

In paying your water company you are paying both for the water coming out of the taps, and the cost of that same water going down the drain. Sometimes, you might not be sending as much of the water you use down the drain as the average household, usually for three possible reasons:

👍 If you have a very large garden or fill a pond or swimming pool

👍 If you have a 'soakaway' (gravel pit outside)

If you have your own cesspit (nice)

If any of these are true for you then you should talk to your water company about a light sewerage rebate.

COUNCIL TAX

Do you pay too much council tax?

You may well think yes, and it could be that you are not only emotionally correct but legally correct too. Many people's properties are wrongly banded due to the arcane system of working out the council tax due on a property.

Check your band against neighbouring properties at **direct.gov.uk**, and if you are in a higher band than similar neighbouring properties you can contact the Valuation Office Agency, **voa.gov.uk**, or in Scotland the Scottish Assessors Association, **saa.gov.uk**, and ask for a banding assessment. Be aware that they could move you into a higher band, so make sure the properties are very similar, and you haven't added an extension or similar which would raise the value of yours over theirs.

Before you contact the VOA, you should also check actual prices of sales in 1991 – there is a calculator on **moneysavingexpert.com** where you can do this. If the VOA do decide you are in the wrong band you should be refunded the difference since you moved into the property or until the banding was introduced in 1991, whichever is the earlier.

BROADBAND SAVINGS

Cheap landline, TV and broadband packages

There are a huge number of different packages and prices for getting home phone, TV and broadband, and it can be very confusing to know which is the best option for you, and time-consuming making a switch. And although your service shouldn't be affected, many of the companies have quite a poor record on this, and certainly you will have to wait in for an appointment for them to come and set the service up, so consider carefully if it's worth it before making the switch.

Check out a price comparison website, such as **top10.com**, *to find out the package deals available in your area.*

Before you make the switch:

👍 Check the small print of any package, e.g. is your download capacity restricted or unlimited, how much extra are additional set-top boxes etc.

👍 Be wary of switching too quickly – if you are tied into a contract with your current provider (contracts of eighteen months are typical) there will be a fee to pay for leaving early; you may also have to pay for the equipment of theirs that you have

👍 Check if the new provider will charge you a fee for switching to them – this 'migration fee' is not entirely gone, so don't let it be forgotten

👍 If you do switch, use a cashback site such as **topcashback.com** or **quidco.com** and switch through them (currently you can get £160 cashback by switching to a full BT package through **topcashback.com**)

When to unbundle

You don't need your landline package and your mobile deal both to have free calls. If one has, take the deal off the other. You can save money by ditching the landline altogether and go for unbundled deals without a landline.

Take Internet meter readings

To work out which broadband deal is the best for you, you need to know how much Internet capacity you actually use and at what times of the day. So go to **thinkbroadband.com** and download their bandwidth meter, tbbmeter, which will track when and how much you use the Internet. (It will not track what you use it for or access any of your personal details.) The cheapest broadband deals limit capacity – if you check your Internet usage, you will know if these deals would work for you.

Stick rather than switch

If you are undecided about facing the hassle that can be involved in switching TV, broadband and phone providers, phone your current provider and say you are thinking of switching and ask them what they can do. They will most likely offer you a better deal than you currently have – either a cheaper package or more bundled services for the same money.

Media for free

👍 There are sites such as **zattoo.com** where you can legally watch TV for free on your computer

👍 Catch up with your favourite TV programmes on dedicated channel websites – BBC iPlayer, 4OD and ITV Player are three such popular sites which allow you to watch programmes you've missed for free

👍 Sign up for radio podcasts so that you never end up hearing a programme, liking it and later paying for CDs of the series or concert

👍 You can listen to thousands of music tracks for free on online radio stations, or if you want to buy music look at **tunechecker.com** to see where you can get it cheapest

CHEAP CALLS

Say no to 0870

And 0845, and 0844, and the whole lot of numbers that sound like they might be free but aren't. Many mobile and landline deals have free calls to landline and mobile phones, but 0870 and 0845 numbers are chargeable – cheaply from landlines, but often extortionately from mobiles (40p a minute is common). The money from calling these numbers goes to the company you are calling, often about a service problem you are having with them. Don't pay these charges; instead go to **saynoto0870.com** and use the search tool at the top of the page to find a genuine landline number for whichever company you need.

Phone for free

Have a phone call or video call anywhere in the world for free with Skype, at **skype.com**, either on your computer or your mobile. Just make sure that everyone you want to talk to also has Skype to avoid any charges.

Cheapest regular phone calls abroad

There are countless adverts and websites advertising the cheapest international calls. The truth is that every company specializes in the cheapest calls to a particular region, so look around to check they are the cheapest for where you want to call. **Moneysavingexpert.com** has an international call checker finding you the cheapest rates for every country – often as low as 1p per minute for many countries in the world. Be aware that it is computer generated, so do check the call company's own website to be sure that rate still applies.

There is no need to buy international calling cards as these call companies are very easy to use – you just dial a special number and the charges simply get billed on your regular phone.

The best mobile deals for you

Research has shown that millions of us are paying £200 a year more than we need to for our mobile bills – most people overspend their monthly allowances, meaning they should move to a higher tariff, and a quarter of people use only a fraction of their allowance, meaning they should be on a lower tariff.

To work out the best deal for you, study your old mobile bills if you are on a monthly contract, and work out what you actually spend and on what. Some companies will provide this information for you if you ring the helpline – but make sure it's a free helpline. Then you know how to structure the best deal for you, i.e. do you make a lot of calls or send a lot of texts? If you are on pay-as-you-go, keep a clear track on how much you top the phone up by, and request free texts from your operator on your usage.

There's an amazing variety of mobile deals out there – different call prices, different contract lengths, cashback, 'free' gifts of laptops or large-screen TVs etc., etc. It is hard to sift through all this choice and decide which package, which phone and which contract is right for you. Looking at some of the mobile-phone comparison websites such as **onecompare.com**, **moneysupermarket.com** or **mobilephonechecker.com** can help, but it can make the choice even more bewildering. The first option is always to ask your current provider, if you have one, if they can do you a better deal – 'press option one if you're thinking of leaving us'.

There are three rules of thumb for getting the cheapest mobile deal:

1. You save money with monthly contract deals over pay-as-you-go deals (except for very low usage).
2. You usually save money if you buy a handset separately. from your mobile phone contract rather than bundled in.
3. There's nothing wrong with not using the latest technology.

Upgrades

Remember, **you don't have to upgrade**! If you are on a monthly contract when your upgrade is due, don't take it but ask the phone company to reduce your monthly bill instead. T Mobile will reduce the bill by £5 as standard each time you don't take an upgrade, and other companies offer similar deals.

If you do want to upgrade but are not due an upgrade on your contract yet, first check with friends if anyone has just upgraded and doesn't want their old phone, which might be more recent than yours. You can also phone your operator and they will usually upgrade you three months before your schedule if you ask them nicely (i.e. threaten to leave).

Coverage

There are only four networks in the UK – Orange/T Mobile, Vodafone, O2 and 3. All the other 'networks' such as One-Tel or even BT Mobile actually use one of these networks. Orange in general has the most widespread coverage, but if you are in a remote area, check which network covers it best. Ofcom shows the locations of all the radio masts so you can find out which network owns the nearest mast to you – visit **sitefinder.ofcom.org.uk**.

Don't call 0800 from a mobile

These calls are free from landlines but very expensive from mobiles. Find the relevant landline number (at **saynoto0870.com**) and call that instead.

Check unused credit if you switch networks

If you do switch networks, the phone operators should credit any unused credit to your new provider, but they mostly don't do so automatically. So, contact them and ask for your credit to be switched over. Mentioning Ofcom's ruling that the phone operators should do this often works wonders.

Sell your old phone, and laptop, and printer cartridges, and ...

Don't let an old phone rust in the drawer – there are many companies that will pay for old, even broken phones because of the valuable components in them. **Mazumamobile.com** guarantees to pay the price it shows on the website for a particular model of phone you send into them, whatever condition it is in. (Other websites list one price on their site but may reduce the amount they actually send to you depending on condition.) **Mazumamobile.com** pays £5 for a five-year-old broken Nokia, so anything newer and actually working goes for a lot more.

Use **mobilevaluer.com** to find out what you could get for all sorts of electrical items, from defunct laptops to old iPods. **Mopay.co.uk** and **weeebuy.co.uk** are owned by the same parent and between the two of them they buy back just about every electrical item you have ever had.

> *Sell your old CDs to* **musicmagpie.co.uk** *– after you've backed them up onto your computer. And sell your old printer cartridges, e.g. to Green Tech Recycle,* **gtrecycle.com***. They pay on average £12 each and the company picks up from your address.*

SUMMARY

You can save £££s by being proactive about your monthly bills – checking you need what you are paying for, and looking out for better deals and switching when you find them. Also manage your home as an asset to you – can you put solar panels on the roof and be paid for the electricity you generate? Can you make or buy a water butt to catch the water your gutters collect which would otherwise be destined for the drain? Sell your old phone, sell your old CDs, check you're not overpaying on council tax and NEVER pay for 0870 numbers.

5. Insurance

SENSIBLE INSURANCE ADVICE

Get yourself covered

Insurance is a good thing. No one agreed with this more than Winston Churchill: at the height of World War Two, he still found time to declaim that there should be 'national compulsory insurance for all classes for all purposes from the cradle to the grave'. But what he didn't mention was that while it's good to get insurance, it's even better to get it for the best price.

Buildings and contents cover

Paying for a year upfront usually makes the total cheaper than if you pay monthly, although often policies with your own bank are not structured this way. So if you can't afford the yearly premium in one go, be sure to check the quote from your own bank.

Get the right cover

Often buildings cover covers more than it needs to, and if so, you could save £££s on your premium. Buildings insurance covers you for the cost of having to rebuild your home in case it is entirely knocked down by, for example, a freak hurricane. So the total amount you are covering for is for the cost of rebuilding, *not* the value of the property. Many people wrongly cover for the property value, costing themselves £££s.

The rebuilding cost is often less than the amount a property would sell for, because it only covers materials and labour and not any location value. Your insurer can make a standard assumption for you based on your property size. For a more accurate picture, the Building Cost Information Service, **bcis.co.uk**, has a calculator which works out what your rebuild cost would be – **calculator.bcis.co.uk**.

Don't underestimate

On the other hand, make sure you have enough cover for contents – it's easy to underestimate what you have and research has shown that one quarter of people who have home insurance don't have enough cover. Most frequently forgotten essentials are carpets, curtains, clothes and cookware. Calculators help you add up what you have and are on many insurers' sites, e.g. **comparethemarket.com**, and Parago Home has launched a phone app to help you note all your possessions easily. Back up your phone online, though, otherwise if that too goes in the flood, your painstaking notes will have been for nothing.

Insurance for your boiler, plumbing etc.

You can go crazy trying to insure against every eventuality. Assess the likelihood of your boiler or drains malfunctioning against the risk that you wouldn't be able to pay for repairs if they did. If you are very risk-averse and you own your own home (this insurance is not necessary for renters) then this kind of home cover could be for you. If so, don't immediately go with the insurance offered by your provider but compare prices, e.g. at **energyhelpline.com** or **moneysupermarket.com**, and also check the price of the biggest provider, **homeserve.com**.

Don't automatically renew

Insurers count on consumers to be apathetic and automatically renew rather than shopping around. Don't let them get away with this.

Get a better deal without comparing

First option for cheaper insurance is to haggle with your current provider and see if they can offer you a cheaper premium – if you compare and find a cheaper quote tell them this, but you can also ask if they can reduce the premium without your having first done the legwork of comparing.

Also check a quote with your bank, as many banks offer special deals for their own customers.

Bundle

You can often get a better deal on home and contents policies by buying them both from the same insurer.

Comparison websites

The many comparison websites are great at shopping around for you. To get the best picture of what's available for your particular circumstances, you should enter your details into several comparison websites as they each cover different insurers. Carefully check the details of cover as the policies will vary, especially the excess you will have to pay if you claim.

Gocompare.com covers the most insurers, then **moneysupermarket.com**, then **comparethemarket.com**, and then **confused.com**, while **uswitch.com** is growing.

> *There are some insurers that refuse to be covered by*
> *any comparison websites so you should check individually*
> *with the best of these – Aviva, which is one of the world's*
> *biggest insurers, and Direct Line. (Intriguingly, this is*
> *owned by the Royal Bank of Scotland, which recently*
> *launched its own price comparison website,*
> **tescocompare.com**.*)*

Be aware: most of the comparison sites are in fact owned by insurance companies, and many insurance companies own other insurance companies, so while it looks like there is massive choice and a huge number of companies, in reality there are only a very few. For example: **Confused.com** is owned by Admiral, **Comparethemarket.com** is owned by Budget, Halifax, esure, Sheila's Wheels and First Alternative are owned by HBOS ... and so on.

This consolidation is in many ways a good thing, as it means that your policy is backed by a major insurance company that you can be reasonably confident can take the strain. But it does mean that each comparison website will show you quotes from the other insurance groups in their stable above all others.

There are some independent price comparison websites, such as **moneysupermarket.com** and **quotezone.co.uk**, and independent specialist insurers are also worth a check for a quote, e.g. Adrian Flux, **adrianflux.co.uk**, for cars; Hiscox, **hiscox.co.uk**, for home contents with high value items.

Buy your insurance through a cashback site, such as **topcashback.com,** *and you could get up to £120 cashback. As ever with cashback sites, don't count the money as yours until you have withdrawn it from the site and it has appeared in your bank account.*

Phone insurance

It's almost always cheaper to add your phone to any home insurance policy you might have than to get a dedicated phone insurance policy.

To buy life cover or not to buy life cover?

Despite its name, this insurance only covers you when you die, i.e. it pays out a sum of money to your inheritors. If you have no dependents then you have no real need for life cover, but if you have children or other dependents then it is wise to have cover in the event of your death. But check if you are already covered – e.g. many employer pension schemes also pay out often quite large death benefits. If not, then **Moneyworld.com** on 0800 118 5115 guarantees to offer the cheapest life cover and has a very low fee of only £25 and no commission.

As there are no extras or options with life cover, there is no reason not to get the very cheapest premium for the same level of cover. Of course to reduce the cost of your cover, you can opt for a smaller payout. Better still, reduce your risk to the insurer, so rule one is: if you want life cover and you smoke, stop.

SUMMARY

Use all the price comparison methods to get yourself the best price possible for all your insurance needs, and check that you don't pay twice on two different insurance policies for the same thing. Make sure you aren't paying too much for insurance because you have the wrong level of cover – e.g. check your buildings insurance covers the cost of re-building your home only, not its value to an estate agent. Add your mobile phone to a home insurance policy rather than buy dedicated cover for it, and, for the best priced life insurance cover, if you smoke – stop.

6. Daily Bread: Where to Shop

SUPERMARKET SHOPPING THE *SAVING* WAY

Don't let the supermarket push your trolley around

Don't let the supermarket be in charge of what you buy with their bright signage and clever store layouts. Instead, plan, plan, plan:

👍 Make a list of what you need

👍 Buy near alternatives to your list that are on special offer

👍 Make a budget for how much you are going to spend and stick to it

> *If, by a miracle of special offers, you go under your budget, put those extra pennies aside, e.g. in a savings wallet you carry round with you.*

Marketing

Beware eye-level marketing. Supermarkets have spent millions on research using eye-tracking technology to learn that we most easily buy things at eye level. And brands have made this research worthwhile by paying to have their products stocked on the shelves just there.

So be aware – those chocolate goodies are right there in front of you because somebody paid for them to be there to tempt you.

Instead of reaching for them look high, look low, and you might see something you actually need for half the price.

They can BOGOF while you keep the savings

Buy one get one free offers can be great – but don't be tempted to consume things twice as fast or buy what you don't need. Put the spare one in the food cupboard or freezer and put those pounds and pennies saved in your savings wallet.

Small is beautiful

Try to shop in a smaller rather than a larger supermarket. Supermarkets lay out their shops to tease you away from your list with popular items spread out – cereal at one end, milk at another. So sticking to your list in a smaller supermarket shop sends you past fewer tempting goodies than in a big supermarket. But do beware – corner shops and 'Express' and 'Metro' versions of supermarkets often price the same goods higher, and also don't offer as much of their range, e.g. if there's no 'Value' option you might pay a higher price than you need.

Time it right

Just as you shouldn't go shopping for fashion when you're feeling unsightly, so don't go shopping for food when you're feeling hungry.

Shop late in the day and you will pick up the deals on bread and fresh fruit and veg which are about to go out of date. Also, there is less of a delicious baking-bread aroma at this time to tempt you into getting more bread and pastries than you ever planned to buy.

Loyalty to yourself, not to a supermarket

Supermarkets differentiate their prices across their goods – e.g. although Tesco famously has a price check campaign and website, **tescopricecheck.com/PriceCheck**, to prove that they are the cheapest, it is of course not true on every product at every time. Patronize more than one supermarket (in every way) in order to get the best offers from each.

> **Mysupermarket.co.uk** *lets you put items in your online shopping trolley and shows you the different prices of them in different supermarkets that day.*

Climbing down their pricing ladder

Supermarkets also offer different prices on almost completely the same goods by creating different branded ranges – premium brands, e.g. Sainsbury's 'Taste the Difference' muffins (31p a muffin), are priced above manufacturers' brands, e.g. Warburton's muffins (22p a muffin), which are themselves priced higher than the supermarket's own brand (18p a muffin) and the supermarket's 'basic' range is the cheapest of all (10p a muffin). In this typical example of price comparison, the supermarket's premium product is more than three times as expensive as its value product. But is it three times as good? Can you really taste the difference that much? You don't need always to buy the very cheapest, but try going down the price ladder at least one rung and see if you can tell the difference. If you can't, stick with it.

> *Supermarkets also sell the same product at different prices in different parts of the shop, e.g. nuts or raisins in the snack section are much more expensive than in the cooking section, so watch out for this.*

Impulse buys

Avoid products that are situated just as you walk in and those by the tills as these are the overpriced impulse buys.

Buying in bulk

Join Costco or get a friend to. Buying in bulk will always give you a better price than buying in small units. Costco has the biggest bulk and so the best deals to be found, and as it expands it is easier to get at them. Costco, **costco.co.uk**, is a chain of twenty-three huge warehouses right across the UK, which sells branded packaged goods at substantially below standard supermarket prices.

You need to join and pay membership (£20 per year) and, as the shops are designed for trade customers, not individuals, you need to justify your application. Being self-employed, or a teacher or doctor, is good enough. Download the application form, bring a business card and £20 to the shop and you can join then and there.

Free with your membership is another card for your partner or nominated friend, and further membership cards only cost £12 each per year – so if a friend is eligible to join, you can buy a card from them, and then you're a member too. Take your car and stock up, but be sure to stick to your list.

Cheap supermarkets

Pile 'em high and sell 'em cheap supermarkets like Aldi, Lidl, Netto and Kwiksave have a lot to recommend them. They used to be characterized as depressing food sheds, but have changed their offers a lot. There are many smaller shops than there were previously, with smaller piles and so greater choice than before, and many are now in town centres. A recent *Which*? survey found these bargain-bucket supermarkets had the happiest customers. Bring your own bags as some of them charge.

> *Keep stocks of staple foods in your cupboards, such as tinned tomatoes, beans, rice, pasta etc., so you don't get caught short and have to run out to the expensive corner shop.*

Bargain

Even supermarkets will bargain with you – if a product is slightly damaged or almost out of date, ask for a reduction. Ask for the manager if the checkout person can't help.

VENTURE BEYOND THE SUPERMARKETS

Catering butchers

Buying meat in larger quantities can save £££s. Either freeze the excess meat to use at a later date or club together with friends or a transition town network (see transition towns in Shopping: Make Technology Work for You chapter, page 14) to make the most of these bulk-buy savings. Look at the National Association for Catering Butchers website to find catering butchers near you – **nacb.co.uk**.

Groceries that are cheap and green

👍 Buy fruit and veg that's in season – it's much cheaper, and better for the environment. And remember, pumpkins are half their price the day after Halloween and Brussels sprouts are a very cheap buy the week after Christmas

👍 Fruit and veg is often much cheaper in a local market than in supermarkets. Often cheaper again is produce from farm shops and houses advertising eggs, jams etc. on country roads. It's much riper too – so be sure to eat within a day or two, or freeze

👍 Soft fruit, e.g. raspberries and blueberries, freeze extremely well, and are delicious as snacks straight from the freezer on a hot day: cheaper and healthier than costly ice cream

👍 If you do buy fruit and veg in supermarkets, produce that you choose and put in bags yourself is often cheaper than pre-packed. But do check – oranges especially are almost always best value pre-bagged

👍 Farmers' markets can sell good food well priced, but before you go, check how much you usually spend on meat or cheese per 100g to ensure you are getting a good deal. More farmers' markets are springing up all the time, visit **farmersmarkets.net** for locations and times of ones near you

If you're not too squeamish, look out for the produce that local fruit and veg markets are planning to throw away. You may be surprised by how acceptable the quality is, and where you have seen produce of its quality before – I know of one corner shop that gets all its fruit this way and sells it on, so making pure profit every time someone buys a banana

SUMMARY

Buy your packaged goods in bulk at Costco and your perishables at the local market and you will save £££s. When in a supermarket, beware the clever marketing tricks they employ to encourage you to buy what *they* want, not what you want. Make sure *you're* pushing your trolley around, and have loyalty to yourself – not to a supermarket.

7. Food Saving in the Home

> 'THE MINT MAKES IT FIRST, IT IS UP TO YOU TO MAKE IT LAST.'

WASTE NOT, WANT NOT

Fridge and storage management

👍 Move food from the fridge that is about to go past its sell-by date into the freezer

👍 Save packaging from cheese so that your next cheese purchase can be double wrapped – don't store cheese just in its single packaging from the shop, as it won't cover all the cheese and the areas exposed to the air will go dry and stale. You can get plastic boxes for free if you buy a takeaway salad/hot food from many bakeries; old ice cream boxes also do an excellent job

👍 Be conscious of consuming food by its use-by date rather than sell-by date. Also remember that use-by dates are there to protect shops from lawsuits just as much as they are there to protect you from mould – if food still looks and smells good enough to eat, it probably is. Use your common sense, though, and don't feed it to anyone very sick, very old or very young

👍 Cheap plastic airtight containers do a better job at keeping bread fresh than swanky bread bins

👍 Don't buy freezer bags – instead re-use the bags from food products from supermarkets or the plastic covers from free magazines

From dregs to riches

👍 Don't throw away the last sips of wine or beer from bottles – put them into ice cube trays to make perfect thimbles of flavour to add to casseroles and stews. (To keep food or drink clean in ice cube trays in the freezer, freeze for a few hours then pop out into plastic bags before they are frozen solid, and then tie up the bag)

👍 Grate stale bread or savoury biscuits to make your own delicious breadcrumbs. Store in an airtight container

👍 Pop old cakes in the blender to make toppings for puddings. Likewise blitz biscuits to make crunchy tops for crumbles

👍 If you cook a duck or goose, roast it on a wire rack that fits over a dish in order to let the fat drain away into the dish while it cooks. Makes the bird taste better and less fatty – and you can then save the fat to cook delicious roast potatoes in another day

Soups, leftovers and gravy

👍 Boil up chicken and fish bones with some veg added in to make stocks for soups, risottos etc. The liquid can then also be frozen in ice cube trays for easy adding to casseroles etc.

👍 Soups are an excellent way to use up vegetables that don't look quite shiny new enough to just boil or steam

👍 When you pour out boiled water from cooking veg, be sure to pour it into a pan or dish that needs a good clean (or save it for gravy and mix in a few gravy granules), not just down the sink; unless it's your sink that needs a good clean, in which case put a bit of bleach (or vinegar or bicarb – see the Cleaning Your Home chapter, page 138) down there first. Just make sure you don't put bleach in the gravy!

👍 Use leftovers – whether it's a cooked dish from last night or bits of cheese and ends of cucumbers left in the fridge. Always reheat food thoroughly, especially rice and chicken, to prevent getting sick. Adding a dash of soya sauce and some fresh cheese to melt on top often transforms a bowl of leftovers popped in the microwave into a yummy-tasting meal

Use the microwave

Microwaves use much less energy to cook many foods than the hob or oven, and you don't need to boil water or wash a pan afterwards. Here are three simple steps to quick and energy-conscious spuds:

1. Wash potatoes if necessary, and pat dry. Score the skins.
2. Put in the microwave on a piece of kitchen towel or a plate and cook seven to eight minutes for three to four medium-sized potatoes.
3. Eat and enjoy.

Top tip: For extra yummy potatoes, use the microwave to par-cook the potatoes, e.g. cooking for four to five minutes for three to four medium-sized potatoes. Then add them to a dish already roasting in the oven or fry for a few minutes for extra crispy tastiness.

Microwave, rather than boil, small portions of vegetables – it uses less energy and keeps the vegetables greener too.

Small is always beautiful

- A little of good things can go a long way – e.g. buy a small amount of parmesan reggiano rather than a whole box of grated parmesan. The flavour is stronger so you need to use less

- Use the smallest saucepans you can and put a lid on while cooking – the food heats quicker using less energy, and takes less water to boil

- Watch portion sizes – do your family or friends actually eat all you're putting on their plates? Do they need to? Carbohydrates – potatoes, rice, pasta – are especially prone to being left on plates. Try not to cook and chuck

Switch to wholewheat pasta: it costs the same as regular pasta but it's more filling so you need less, and it's more nutritious too.

Bag it up

Tea from tea bags tastes just the same when you re-use the bag a second time. Keep it to one side on a clean saucer. For herbal tea, there is no need to use boiling water – save energy by stopping the kettle before it's boiled, then let the tea infuse.

Then compost

If you have a garden, you can compost your vegetable cuttings to make free earthy treats for your plants – some local authorities give out free composters on request. The dos and don'ts of composting are simple:

👍 **Do** put in a good blend of 'browns', i.e. shredded paper, wood shavings/twigs, torn-up egg boxes and some fallen leaves; with 'greens', i.e. tea bags, coffee grounds, vegetable and fruit peelings and grass clippings

👍 **Don't** put in cooked food, meat, weeds or sick plants

Contrary to popular opinion, your composter won't smell except when you open the lid. It also takes almost no effort – don't believe the propaganda which says you have to manage the compost carefully, stir it regularly etc. Just put the stuff in and wait.

Food for less, or for *nothing*

Pick your own fruit in season – at professional pick-your-own places: **pickyourown.info** has a list of what's available and where. This will save you ££s and makes for a fun day out. Even if you live in the heart of a city, you are probably not very far from some rambling bushes from where you can pick delicious fruit and veg such as blackberries, blueberries, elderflower, damsons, rose hips, hazlenuts, sweet chestnuts, mushrooms, garlic and nettles. The countryside is awash with this stuff; in cities look along canal routes and any heaths or wild parkland.

> *For tips on what to look for and what to do with the produce once you've picked it (and how not to die of mushroom poisoning), look at* **hedgerowharvest.org.uk** *and* **mushrooms.org.uk**. *Always give hedgerow food a good wash before you eat it.*

Grow your own

- 👍 Start small for easy gratification. You don't need to buy a cress-growing kit; cress seeds will grow on a watered piece of fabric or half an eggshell (painting a face on encourages kids)

- 👍 You can use a window ledge to grow herbs – basil grows well from seed, and a piece of mint will root in water and then you can plant it out. 'Cut and come again' varieties of lettuce grow well from seed and provide almost constant salad – you cut and eat some lettuce leaves and the plant re-grows, making more

- 👍 Buying from seeds is always cheaper than buying plants

- 👍 Runner beans grow well in most soils and can grow up walls. Plant seeds in old toilet rolls filled with soil or compost (e.g. John Innes No. 1) and then plant out when they've grown a little

- 👍 If you have no garden but a wall or front door, you can grow tumbling tomatoes in a hanging basket (Tumbling Tom variety is good)

- 👍 There is no need to buy pots to grow vegetables or fruit – you can use old bins or boxes, or a pile of car tyres. Spare wheelie bins make great growers – and they can be wheeled inside or under shelter if the weather turns inclement. We favour growing things in old shoes or boots. Paint them up to look pretty and plant – that's it. Collapsible planters are great for veg planting because they fold away to nothing after harvest time – see your local garden centre or **amazon.co.uk**

👍 Use the conditions you have – herbs don't need very much sun, but tomatoes do. Potatoes, carrots, onions, broad beans, strawberries and raspberries are all easy growers – they just need good soil and watering

👍 Get an allotment, perhaps with a friend to share the workload

👍 Join a community allotment or community orchard – you all pitch in when you can to help grow the food, and then you all get to pick and eat at harvest time. You can get free seeds, do seed swaps and benefit from others' expertise. Check out **communityhelpers.co.uk** or find your local transition town, **TransitionNetwork.org**

👍 When you're serious about the Good Life, buy chickens for gorgeous fresh eggs every day for little trouble: see **poultry.allotment.org.uk** for all you need to know

Dine and drink at home

Staying in and cooking at home will save you £££s on eating out. You often get better drink this way too, and if you are lucky enough to be or know a good chef, the food can also be better.

👍 For dinner parties, the easy way is to suggest that everyone brings a course – this shares the cost and the hassle of cooking

👍 Make sure you choose your menu carefully – cook dishes with cheap ingredients that easily produce large amounts of food, such as a bean chilli, chickpea curry or vegetable soup. Resist the temptation to whip up dishes featuring expensive delicacies – especially if you're catering for lots of guests

👍 If no one can face cooking, you can get great restaurant food at home for less – many restaurants do takeaways for less than their eat-in prices, even if they don't advertise the fact. Don't be afraid to ask

👍 Most supermarkets have 'dinner for two for £10' or similar deals which are good value if you like their food

👍 Bulk shops such as Majestic can do good deals on wine, but often the supermarkets will do the very best deals as long as you choose carefully – look out for any favourite you have and only buy it when it's on special offer

Go veggie (at least sometimes)

On average we eat more meat than is ideal for our bodies and not enough veg. Switch this around and you will save £££s – a vegetarian diet can be much cheaper than a meat diet, and you could save money on health costs too.

Make your own

There are countless delicious food items that are easy and enjoyable to make at home, and you'll also have the great advantage of knowing exactly what's in them:

DRINKS – buy cranberry concentrate for £2 from a health food shop and make litres of delicious cranberry juice.

(Shop-bought cranberry juice is made exactly this way, with around 75% water.) Make your own yummy ginger beer at a cost of several pence, see **ehow.com**. You can make countless liqueurs from wild picked sloes, elderflower etc. See **CottageSmallHolder.com** for hundreds of ideas.

HOT CHOCOLATE POWDER – commercial chocolate powders are made with only around 20% cocoa, and are 75% sugar! Not to mention the added salt and other flavourings. Cut the sugar, ditch the salt, and halve the cost by buying cocoa powder and adding sugar to your own desired quantity.

DRIED FRUIT – buy quantities of fruit, e.g. plums, apricots and peaches, cheaply when they are in season and home dry them, see **seasonalchef.com** for how. Then save ££s on the prices charged in shops for dried fruit. You also now have ingredients for homemade muesli – better for you and much, much cheaper. Add to your dried fruit with nuts from big cheap packs (not the overpriced snack packs).

BREAD – you can go the whole hog and make your own bread – utterly delicious but it does take a while and you do tend to over-eat as it's so divine and fresh. A cheap and easy alternative is to make bread from the pre-mixed flour and yeast packs sold in supermarkets. Divide up the bag as the quantity each pack makes is large.

ICE CREAM – professional ice cream makers cost hundreds of pounds, but for just £20 you can buy the 'ice cream ball' and after twenty minutes of rolling a crazy coloured plastic ball, you can make delicious ice cream by using only cream, sugar, vanilla or fruit (if desired), ice and (wait for it) salt. Don't worry: the salt doesn't go in the mixture, it simply lowers the freezing point of the ice to make it colder thus turning the cream to ice cream. Check out **icecreamrevolution.com** for advice, recipes and where to buy the amazing device.

SUMMARY

Wasting food wastes money too. On average, UK households throw away 20% of the food they buy – households with children throw away almost 30%. Better food management in the fridge and cupboards, cutting down on the carbs on people's plates, and finding new uses for old bread and biscuits can really reduce how much you waste. Picking your own food from hedgerows and growing your own food, whether in your garden, a window box or a community allotment can save you £££s. And then you can make your own delicious prepared food from these fresh ingredients – you will save packets.

8. Money: Saving for You

> 'ANNUAL INCOME TWENTY POUNDS, ANNUAL EXPENDITURE
> NINETEEN POUNDS NINETEEN AND SIX, RESULT HAPPINESS.
> ANNUAL INCOME TWENTY POUNDS, ANNUAL EXPENDITURE TWENTY
> POUNDS OUGHT AND SIX, RESULT MISERY.'
>
> **MR MICAWBER FROM *DAVID COPPERFIELD***

TAKE CONTROL

Get active

Be in charge of your money. The first step to better financial health is working out exactly how much spare income you have, or don't have. So, even if you are scared of numbers, or of the cold hard realities of your monetary situation, you need to grasp the nettle and find out the facts.

The facts

Most of us are paid our income into a bank account in a lump sum each month, which can give the illusion of spare spending money over and above the rent/mortgage. But beware – before you can make an accurate assessment of spare spending money, you need to budget for all the regular payments you can predict but can't avoid, like council tax, gas, food etc., as well as the less regular payments that are more difficult to predict, but also unavoidable, like holiday spending, birthday presents, and so on.

So that you don't get surprised when Christmas comes along and you need money for presents and parties, and so that you aren't then surprised a second time by the January sales coming straight after Christmas (as they will do every year!) when you will need money to buy efficiently in the sales, you *must* budget.

> *Don't think of the January sales as simply being for shopaholics. Primarily, they are for bargain-hunters. The crowds can be off-putting, but just think of the money you could save by buying essential, need-to-have items at a massive discount.*

Make a simple budget

These words may put the fear of goodness-knows-what into some readers, but it's really not that tricky. You can find budget-making tools to work out what you spend each month on websites such as **free-financial-advice.net**, but the problem with these is that you have to guess so many expenses, e.g. how much do you spend per month on cleaning products?

One place to start is to ask for an appointment with your bank – they will help you go through your spendings for the last few months for free.

> *When discussing your financial matters with any financial specialist, don't let them fool you with complicated language – they should be able to explain everything to you in language that you understand. As Einstein said: if you can't explain it simply, you don't understand it well enough.*

Working out the unknown expenses

👍 Either get a budget app on your phone or use a tool online, e.g. at **confused.com**: you put in your bank balance and then just enter the amount you're spending every time you buy something or pay a bill, and it will work out the rest that's left for you

👍 Or simply carry round a notebook and pen with you and jot down what you spend each time in the categories from the table on page 74

Do this for a month, adding in all the monthly direct debits (e.g. mortgage, savings etc. – check your bank account to find out what these are, as there are often more than you think), plus one third of the quarterly bills (e.g. gas, electricity), and a twelfth of the annual bills (e.g. water) and you'll then have a really accurate picture of where your money goes and which expenses need to be slimmed down if you want to have more of it.

But remember some spending is seasonal, e.g. electricity and gas bills are higher in the winter, so it's best for these to add up the bills for the year if possible, and then divide by twelve to get the spending for each month.

> *And don't forget all the tiny expenses – the occasional stamp, the odd bus ride – as Benjamin Franklin said, 'Beware of little expenses; a small leak will sink a great ship.'*

The really tricky yearly spendings

The big killer for any budget is making sure you add in the spendings that you will make each year to the amount you have to budget for each month. Some are hard to remember but easy to work out the cost of, e.g. annual National Trust membership or yearly breakdown cover. So check the table below to make sure you've got them all down.

Some expenses are easy to remember but hard to work out the cost of, e.g. Christmas, holidays, spending on birthdays. Guessing is better than giving up! Better still is to work out how much you think you should be spending on these through the year, and then try to stick to that. Then when Christmas or a holiday comes around, use your notebook or phone app adder to track whether you do achieve this budget.

A ready reckoner to work out your spare money

Track your spending for a month, add in those tricky yearly costs, and you have a result that should look like the table over the page:

Actual monthly spending	£
Monthly spendings on essentials:	
Home – rent/mortgage, insurance (home, contents, personal [including life], pet, car and travel), council tax, monthly amount for water, gas, oil and electricity bills, TV/broadband/telephone bills	
Food and shopping essentials – food shopping, meals at work, pet food, other home shopping e.g. cleaning products, toiletries	
Debt payments – student loan, personal loan, HP loan and credit card repayments	
Education spending – courses and classes	
Clothes and shoes essentials	
Transport – bus, train, coach, taxi, car (maintenance, tax, petrol)	
Savings – saving schemes, pension payments, investments	
Family – childcare, play schemes, school dinners, pocket money, clothes, nappies/wipes	
Newspapers or magazines	
Other (list)	

Monthly discretionary spendings:	
Mobile phone – you could argue this is discretionary or essential …	
Books, music, gadgets, clothes, hobbies, computer games, treats, plants/flowers	
Going out – spending in pubs, restaurants, cafes, cinemas etc., plus any babysitting costs and transport costs (e.g. taxi)	
Staying in – drinks for home, luxuries e.g. chocolates, rental DVDs, takeaways	
Health and beauty – haircuts, beauty treatments, contact lenses	
Other (list)	

Yearly spendings: (divided by twelve to give monthly amount)	£
Christmas	
January sales	
Holidays	
Birthdays	
Car tax, breakdown cover, TV licence	
Annual memberships, charity donations	
House and garden maintenance	
Health – prescriptions or prescription prepayments, dentistry, opticians, cold remedies	
Big ticket items – e.g. new kitchen, house re-decoration, new car	
Other (list)	

Total outgoings	£

Actual monthly income (after tax)	£
Average monthly income from employment or self-employment	
Income from savings or investments	
Income from pensions	
Benefits (e.g. child benefit, housing benefit)	
Total	£

Take one total away from the other to see how much less, or more, than your income you spend.

DON'T PANIC!
Whatever the outcome, knowledge is power and now that you know the worst, you can do something about it.

Specifically three things:

1. Reduce the monthly home, electricity, food shopping etc. bills by using the tips in the rest of this book.
2. Reduce your discretionary spending – see which discretionary spend you make most shocks you with how much it adds up to, and try to do something about it, either by reducing its cost or the amount of it you consume.
3. Actively manage your money to get the best deals on mortgages, savings etc., and also make a plan to save for the big ticket yearly items.

Actively managing your money

Many people are scared of this but it's not as hard as it sounds. It's all about knowing what deals you have at the moment, subscribing to alerts that show you the best deals around (e.g. **moneysavingexpert.com** or **moneysupermarket.com**), and switching if you can do better. Your bank is only your bank if they serve you well, if someone else can serve you better, then switch.

Your finances are your business, but if you have a family, your partner's finances are also your business. Talk openly about your financial situations and try actively to plan your financial future together.

GET THE RIGHT BANK ACCOUNT

Switching your bank account

The days of misguided loyalty to your bank account should be long gone. The fees and benefits of bank accounts vary hugely, and since switching has been made much easier now that banks are able to transfer all your direct debits for you, it pays to look around to see if there is a bank account better for your circumstances than your current one, and if there is, switch.

Use money comparison websites to find what the banks have to offer, but first work out what you are looking for:

👍 If you are regularly overdrawn then look for cheaper overdraft rates and lower fees for exceeding an agreed overdraft, but without paying a monthly fee for the account

👍 If you are always in credit then look for banks which offer the highest interest rate for a standard current account

👍 If you travel abroad often then look for a bank which has credit or debit cards which don't incur any charges for taking out cash abroad, e.g. the Halifax

👍 Start using free alerts from your bank. Some banks like Lloyds TSB and Natwest have bank accounts that send you free text alerts when you get near your overdraft limit, or when you get near a level of spending that you have set

If you are paying for your current account you should almost certainly SWITCH NOW.

Mutuals – ditching your bank account

If you don't like the idea that the interest that your money makes while sitting in the bank is creamed off for the banks' shareholders, then mutuals are for you. The idea behind these is as old as the hills and is brilliant – mutuals have no shareholders, but are collectively owned by everyone who has a stake, which is to say an account, in the business. They also often do very competitive rates for savings, and for loans. The two best ones for coverage across the country, service and good rates are the Co-operative bank and Nationwide.

Check the small print

Banks are in competition for your current account and so you will often see tempting deals – £100 sign-up bonuses are common. But check the small print and be sure that the £100 cashback won't be swallowed up by the first overdraft fee, for example. Often you won't even get the cashback at all if you don't have any direct debits to transfer.

If you do switch, keep the old bank account open with a small balance in for any cheques which haven't gone through yet, or any direct debits that the bank didn't correctly transfer. Otherwise you could end up paying charges, or battling with the bank to get them to pay them.

SAVINGS

Help yourself to save – create different accounts

This way of looking after your money is called piggy banking, and it can really help you save. You can open as many regular savings accounts as you like and you can nominate them for different things – Christmas, holidays, rainy day, etc. Check for the latest best deals on a money comparison site and open accounts to put a little away each month.

Don't expect to earn very much interest on the money, though, even if you get one of the best rates, because you are adding to the amounts each month and so the interest gradually builds up rather than accruing as if you had invested a lump sum. Accounts without easy access, e.g. only one withdrawal a year, are good protection against temptation. Note down when the high interest rate period ends and switch to another deal at that time.

Always check the deals from the government-backed National Savings and Investments as they often have the best savings offers and they are virtually risk free – see **nsandi.com**.

Use your ISA allowance first

Always use your ISA allowance before you think of saving any other way because you never have to pay tax on any interest you earn on an ISA account. Check out the best cash ISA rates, e.g. at **money.co.uk**, and then make sure they are flexible ISAs, which allow you to put money in each month via a direct debit or payment transfer. Unfortunately you can only have one ISA so you can't piggy bank quite so easily, but it's worth it for the tax you save.

To piggy bank using your ISA allowance, work things out this way:

- If you want to spend £900 on holidays in the year, then you need to save £75 each month to afford that

- If it's £150 on Christmas, then that's another £12.50 that needs to be saved each month

- And for a £300 rainy day fund, that would be an extra £25 per month

So if you can start saving £112.50 per month then your piggy banks are set up even though they are all in the same account, and you know you will have your budgeted amounts available to you. Then you just have to stick to your budgets.

Look after the pennies

Whenever you get a BOGOF (buy one get one free) or a '50% extra free' deal, take that money you've just saved out of your wallet and squirrel it away in a savings purse in your other pocket. This way you're actually saving rather than just theoretically saving. Don't get the wallets mixed up though.

Cash in the pennies

Don't use the machines in supermarkets into which you feed your hundreds of 2p coins saved in a jar and they give you back shiny pound coins, because they keep 12p in every £1 they give back. Instead feed the coins into a self-checkout till and every penny will go towards something for you.

LONG-TERM SAVINGS

Pension savings are for now, not just for the future

The most important rules about saving for your pension are that you should do it, and you should do it as soon as you can. The only reason to delay is if you have expensive debts, e.g. credit card balances, in which case it is more efficient to pay these off first before you save elsewhere. But otherwise start now because time is money. Specifically, money invested in pension type products doubles, very roughly depending on the interest rate, every fifteen years. So if you start saving when you're twenty-five, the money you invested at the start can double twice by the time you are fifty-five, whereas if you start when you are forty-five, it doesn't even double once until you are sixty.

Get someone else to chip in

The next most important rules about pensions:

👍 If you have a company pension scheme available to you, you should almost always pay into that before you think about any other private pension scheme

👍 If you are not eligible for a company pension scheme, e.g. because you are self-employed, then get a stakeholder pension

With both of these schemes, you contribute some money to your pension, and someone else contributes some more on your behalf. With the employer schemes it's your employer who pays in (can be up to an extra whopping 60%), and with a stakeholder pension the government chips in an extra 20%.

SUMMARY

Your bank may hold your money but it doesn't necessarily hold your best interests at heart – make sure you are getting a good deal from your bank account, and if you aren't, switch, preferably to a mutual so there aren't any shareholders creaming off your profits. If you have any money to invest, put it in an ISA before you put it anywhere else. Plan your monthly budget without panicking, squirrel away the pennies from the supermarkets' BOGOFs, and start saving for your pension right now.

9. Mortgage and House Rental Savings

FIND THE RIGHT MORTGAGE

Check the paperwork

If you have a mortgage this is by far the biggest financial decision you have to make and getting the very best deal could save you ££££s every year. If you haven't changed your mortgage in a few years, chances are that its initial attractive interest rate has expired and you are now paying a much higher rate that you could slash by switching providers. But do check the paperwork of your original deal to ensure there are no financial penalties for moving within a certain time period.

If this is your first mortgage the whole house-buying process can seem so daunting that getting the best mortgage deal might not be your highest priority, but doing so could save you bucketloads of cash.

Which type of mortgage?

👍 The more you can put down in a deposit the less you will have to pay in interest to the bank

👍 Fixed-rate mortgages are good options if interest rates are likely to rise, whereas variable rate mortgages are best to go for if interest rates are likely to fall (check the latest pronouncements from the Bank of England's monetary policy committee for the prognosis)

👍 Interest only mortagegas are attractive (as the payments are less) but worrying as you need a separate investment to pay off the capital. Best avoided unless you really know what you are doing

👍 Offset mortgages are good for those rare people who have large credit balances, but for mere mortals they are not much use, and usually charge higher interest rates

Finding a mortgage

👍 The comparison websites do a good job in finding a mortgage to suit your particular needs – **moneysupermarket.com**, **moneyextra.com**, **charcol.com** and **moneynet.co.uk**

👍 You can also look at sites just showing the best mortgage deals, but these won't be tailored for your requirements – look at **moneyfacts.co.uk**, or **knowyourmoney.co.uk**

👍 You could use a mortgage broker: some charge a fee, so choose one which works on commission paid by the lender of the money, i.e. not you. London & Country, **lcplc.co.uk**, is a well-established fee-free mortgage broker

If you are a first-time buyer, be sure you make the mortgage company aware of it to take advantage of governmental support for first-time buyers.

Shop around for the add-ons

It's easy to think that your best mortgage provider deal will also give you the best deals on home insurance, life cover etc. They most probably won't. And note that mortgage brokers are obliged to offer independent advice regarding mortgage deals, but not for these add-ons.

See the Buying Your Home chapter for other money-saving tips (page 125).

Overpay on your mortgage

If you have any spare money (!) and you can afford to pay off more of your mortgage than just your fixed monthly repayments, then you will save money on the interest you pay on your mortgage, which adds up to ££££s over the years. Plus you can get a better interest rate if the loan to value (LTV) drops below a particular amount. Better rates usually kick in when you borrow less than 75% of the property's value, and better again with less than 60%. But check you won't incur a penalty – some mortgages have fixed amounts they will let you overpay so be sure to stick to those limits.

Use up your ISA allowance first – only overpay if you have already used up your ISA allowance for savings.

RENT

Reduce your rent

👍 Negotiate with your landlord about the level of your rent and give them reasons to lower the rent for you – for example, offer to maintain the garden, or re-decorate rooms yourself

👍 Discuss with them improvements that you notice need doing and offer to undertake them yourself, or not have them done, for a reduction in the rent

👍 Benchmark the rent with that of comparable properties and if yours is more, bring this up with the landlord and ask for a reduction

👍 If you live in a block of flats where the block is run by a single landlord, check for vacancies in other flats in the block. When they come up, this is the perfect time to arrange a meeting with your landlord to talk about lowering your rent

Make sure that you always pay your rent on time and keep the property in good condition for your landlord to want to accommodate you in this way.

SUMMARY

Your mortgage is most likely your biggest monthly outgoing so make sure you actively manage it. Think carefully about your circumstances and how they might change to make sure that you get the mortgage that is right for you, and then compare the different offers out there. If you can overpay on your mortgage you can save £££s but make sure you won't incur a penalty. If you rent, make sure you keep the property lovely, offer to paint rooms and upkeep the garden, and if you ask nicely (and check neighbouring rents) you might get a rent reduction.

10. Making Money

FINDING MONEY

Literally

You too could rake in a massive haul of Roman coins worth over £1 million, as Dave Crisp did – with only a little investment in a metal detector and a huge amount of time spent scouring the earth listening for little beeps. Check out **garysdetecting.co.uk** for advice on getting started, but don't expect quick success.

Are you the heir to a fortune?

It's not very likely, but worth checking. Banks hold billions of pounds in unclaimed 'orphan' assets. Find out if some of them rightly belong to you from the Unclaimed Assets Register, **uar.co.uk**.

Have you won a prize?

Check whether any unclaimed prizes might actually be yours – at **national-lottery.co.uk**, and at the National Savings and Investments, **nsandi.com**, for premium bonds.

Charity grants

Buy the *Charities Digest* handbook second-hand, e.g. from **Amazon.co.uk**, for £1–2 and search through it to see if there could be a charity which exists to give out grants to precisely people like you. You'd be surprised to find the range of people who are eligible for grants for a whole range of things. There is no need to buy the current edition which costs over £35, as a copy of the book that's a couple of years old will very likely do just as well.

Alternative finance

Credit Unions are non-profit-making co-operatives which pay interest on savings and provide low-cost loans. They are designed for people on low incomes who might otherwise not have access to regular financial savings and loans products. They are regulated by the FSA and so are protected by the safety net of the Financial Ombudsman and Financial Compensation Scheme if things go wrong. See the Association of British Credit Unions, **abcul.org**, for more details.

Are you claiming everything you are entitled to?

👍 **BENEFITS**: Be sure that you are receiving all the government benefits your circumstances entitle you to. Use the benefit checker on **turn2us.org.uk** to find out

👍 **COUNCIL TAX**: Students pay no council tax – even a whole house full of them. Or if you live alone you are entitled to a 25% discount in council tax. If your property is empty and unfurnished, e.g. while undergoing redecoration, you don't need to pay council tax during this period. In all cases, make sure you tell the council as soon as the entitlements start, and again when they end, so that you don't end up having to repay

👍 **HOME AND ENERGY GRANTS**: You may be eligible for a grant to insulate your home or provide you with a new boiler etc. See the Home Improvements chapter for what you could claim for

BURSARIES FOR PRIVATE SCHOOLS: Many private and public schools have bursaries for people in particular financial situations – you don't necessarily need to be on a very low income to be able to qualify. Search for bursaries at **independentschools.com** to find out the options, and look at **FeeAssistanceLondonSchools. org.uk** for London independent schools, or ask a school you are interested in directly

A LITTLE BIT ON THE SIDE

'I'm living so far beyond my income that we may almost be said to be living apart,' said E. E. Cummings. Don't be like him: there are lots of ways of making a little, or a lot, of extra money on the side when you know where to look for them.

Be a mystery shopper

Shops and restaurants are keen to find out if their customer service really makes the grade, and so they will pay for you to buy their goods or eat their food and find out. They sometimes pay in cash which can be up to £50 a day, but more often in vouchers. Most assignments are short and you need to pay for your own travel. Check out **retaileyes.co.uk**, **retail-maxim.co.uk**, **grassrootsmysteryshopping.com** and **mystery-shoppers.co.uk**, and **consumerintelligence.com** to check up on call centres. For restaurant meals for free look at **secretsquirrels.biz** or **mysterydining.com**.

Win a competition

There are hundreds of competitions going on all the time – from single bingo and missing word competitions, to competitions giving prizes to the best photo, or poem, or caption etc. Check out **loquax.co.uk** to find a list of them and how to enter. Avoid pay-to-enter competitions.

Be a TV extra

Being an extra – sorry, I mean 'background artiste' – is not just for Ricky Gervais: you can be one too. You can earn up to £80 a day, although travel expenses are often not paid for. The work is irregular and involves lots of waiting around, but can be great fun. The agencies **2020casting.com** and with **universalextras.co.uk** are free to register but take a cut, while you have to pay to register with sites such as **filmextras.co.uk** and **extras.co.uk**, although the latter has a thirty-day free trial. Upload well shot photographs of yourself to maximize your chances of work.

BE PAID FOR GIVING YOUR OPINIONS

This can be a nice little earner – a good little bit of extra money on the side. There are many ways to do this.

Online survey sites

You can earn little but often by filling in online surveys; vouchers are more common than cold hard cash. The surveys can take just a few minutes to fill in and with most sites you need to reach a threshold before they pay out at all, so only start if you mean to carry on. Sites to look at include **mysurvey.com**, **justtheanswer.co.uk**, **panelbase.net**, **qnaresearch.com** (IT specialists), **onepoll.com** and **valuedopinions.co.uk**.

Be sure to sign up to an extra email address, e.g. at **gmail.com,** *before you start so that you can keep track of the tasks in hand, and so that your regular email account doesn't become entirely clogged.*

Review your holiday

Some travel sites pay for travel reviews from self-styled experts, so if you have a story to tell, especially if it's from an unusual location, then you might be able to make something from it. Check out **simonseeks.com** and, for even more committed wannabe travel writers, **travelintelligence.com**.

Review other products

Brands always want to know how to improve their products, and maybe you have the know-how to tell them. You could always get them to send you their product for free and give it a try – check out **dooyoo.co.uk** who pay up to 60p for each product review you write, and you get to keep the product too. Unless it's a chocolate bar, in which case you get to eat it.

Be in a focus group

You can make good money this way – up to £50 an hour – just by saying what you think on any given subject. The market research companies will restrict how many focus groups you can be in, otherwise there is a danger of overweighting all focus groups with your, no doubt wonderful, opinions. Try **sarosresearch.com**, **fieldinitiatives.co.uk**, **indiefield.co.uk**, and **focus4people.com**.

MAKE MONEY FROM YOUR HOUSE

Rent a room

The government's rent-a-room scheme means that you pay no tax on any income from renting out a room, or a sofa, in your house up to the first £4,250 you make on it in a year. This means not only is it more financially attractive than ever to have a lodger, but also the tax relief has spawned websites which aim to link your room up with potential renters, e.g. **airbnb.com** and **crashpadder.com**. You name your price for a night's stay in your bijou reclining wicker chair in a dingy basement (or possibly your penthouse suite with self-contained towel rail), and if anyone takes the bait they have to pay at least a deposit upfront and the remainder upon arrival (or they can opt to pay fully upfront) and then the website takes a cut of the profit.

Have a foreign exchange student to stay and show them around

For hosting a foreign exchange student (or someone from overseas who wants to improve their English), and providing B&B, you can earn upwards of £80 a night – more if you're offering ensuite accommodation, and yet more if you provide an evening meal and take them out on 'cultural' trips and teach them English for a few hours a day.

Ask at any language schools near you (search the Yellow Pages or **yell.com** *to find them) or take a look at* **interstudies.org.uk**, **homestaybooking.com** *or* **foreignexchangestudent.com**.

Hire out your house or car as a film location

You can get over £1,000 a day for renting out your house or car for a film shoot: we got £500 from a film company to hire our clapped-out old Lada for a day (it was painted tartan at the time). You can register with a bunch of film location companies, but be prepared for quite an amount of disruption if the inside of your house is chosen – outside shots pay out less but involve a great deal less hassle.

There are many film location companies to register with, e.g. **film-locations.co.uk**, **locations-uk.com**, **locationworks.com**, **unitbase.co.uk**, **amazingspace.co.uk**, or for Scotland **scottishscreenlocations.com**.

Sell, sell, sell! And hire out

Get rid of your excess stuff for good – sell it on eBay or at car boot sales. (See Shopping: When and Where to Shop for tips on eBay buying and selling.) Or hire out what you don't need right now but might need some time in the future – check out the peer-to-peer hire site **ecomodo.com** and post online the contents of your shed to see if anyone might be willing to pay to borrow them for a while.

Make money from your car, or driveway

If you have a driveway or other off-road parking and you live in a city where there are parking restrictions, or if you live near any major transport hub such as an airport, you may be able to make money by renting out your parking spot to other drivers. Take a look at the websites **parkatmyhouse.com**, **yourparkingspace.co.uk** and **parkonmydrive.com** to see if it could be for you.

If you have a car which you don't need every day, you could register it as available for rental from **whipcar.com** –

a peer-to-peer car rental site which links you with people who need a car to rent. If your insurance covers other drivers your insurance should not be affected, but do check.

Or your garden

If you would be happy to have people sleep in your garden with occasional use of your house (i.e. for bathroom, kitchen etc.) then check out **campinmygarden.com** and sign up to have your lawn listed.

SUMMARY

There are hundreds of ways to make a little extra money each month – from Internet surveys to mystery shopping, being an extra in a TV show, or renting out your car or garden. Or you might just find money lying around in the ground in the shape of original Roman coins – if you look for long enough. You might already be the heir to a fortune, and wouldn't it be a shame if you never checked to make sure?

11. Credit Cards and Debt Management

> 'MONEY IS BETTER THAN POVERTY, IF ONLY FOR FINANCIAL REASONS.'
>
> **WOODY ALLEN**

CREDIT CARDS

What credit cards are good for

The golden rule when it comes to credit cards is always to pay off the monthly balance in full. This way you will avoid the swingeing rates of interest that credit cards are infamous for. Credit cards are like the girl with the curl in the middle of her forehead – when they are good they are very, very good, but when they are bad they are horrid. Credit cards are very good for three things:

1. Credit cards provide you with short-term debt for free which allows you to spend next month's salary this month. By using balance transfers cleverly, credit cards can give you free debt for longer than this – often up to 18 months.
2. Spending on plastic can get you money back on every purchase if you have the right card. This is a fantastic benefit and it's worth making as many of your regular purchases on your card as possible, **as long as you are certain you can pay off the balance in full**.

3. Buying with a credit card gives you protection over purchases – if you pay for something that costs over £100 with a credit card (*not* with a debit card) then by law the credit card company is jointly liable with the retailer for consumer rights. This means that if the company that made the product goes bust and you need redress, your credit card company is liable for the full cost of the item, and in fact this is true even if you only pay for a tiny amount of the item (e.g. 50p) with your credit card.

What credit cards are bad for

Credit cards can be absolutely horrid if you only pay the minimum repayment each month rather than paying off the balance in full. Even a small balance will result in you paying the credit card company a frightening amount of money by the time the debt is paid off, especially for cards with high APR rates, such as store cards. These are often the easiest to apply for but have the worst, i.e. highest, interest rates for repaying the loan.

So, for example, several major high street chain store cards charges 20% APR, rising to 30% APR if you have a poor credit history. See how a small purchase can ratchet up the debt, and rather take away the shine from the 10% discount you got on the purchase by buying it with your store card.

Imagine you bought something from MadeUpHighStreetShopName with a price of £110. Your store card gives you a 10% discount, so it would only cost you £99. Sounds a good deal? But if you pay off only the minimum £5 each month, it would take you two years to pay back that £99 and it would have cost you an extra £20 in interest. Not such a good deal. And this is assuming your credit history has earned you the 20% APR; if you are on the 30% APR deal, it would take you two and a quarter years to pay off that debt, and cost £33 in interest. Now that's a really bad deal.

So ... Pay off the balance in full every month

If you can't do this, then at least pay off a fixed amount rather than the credit card company's minimum. Also be aware that the higher the interest rate on a card, usually the lower is the minimum payment – so tying you into debt for longer. With your £99 purchase, if you pay a fixed amount of £20 per month (four times a standard minimum payment of £5), you pay off the full amount in six months at a cost of £5 interest. That actually makes the 10% discount worth something – specifically it's worth 5%, and a lot of hassle working out how much fixed payment you need to make, and then setting up the direct debit with your bank (not always straightforward as the form is designed to draw you towards the minimum payment option).

If you do set up a fixed payment, write the amount on a covering letter to protect yourself if they in fact put you on the minimum payment scheme.

Most people don't pay off the balance each month – make sure you do

Moneysupermarket.com has found that almost half of all people with credit cards in the UK don't pay off their balance in full, and the average debt is ten months before the borrowing is paid off. This means that, between all of us in the UK, we are collectively wasting £2.3 billion a year in interest payments that we are giving to those credit card companies because we love them so much.

When easy isn't good

Credit card companies are also alarmingly accomplished at suckering you into spendings that you shouldn't make for things you possibly don't need, in the belief that 'your flexible friend' will pick up the tab. It won't. However quick and easy the credit card transaction is compared with checking your bank balance and then carrying around wads of cash, it's that same money of yours that has to pay the bill at the end of the day, or rather month.

This is another reason to avoid store cards, with their 'special promotional evenings' that lead you to think you're a VIP with privileged access to something exciting, whereas in fact you're a person with a store card about to give more of your hard-earned money to that store.

Cash advances are a disaster

And credit cards are terrible for cash advances – fees of 3% of the cash you withdraw are typical. So the amount you have taken out plus the 3% fee goes onto your balance and adds to the amount you are charged interest on. And, as if that weren't enough, you're typically charged a higher interest rate on the balance that comes from the cash withdrawal!

Hidden fees

Credit cards are notorious for having hidden fees that you might get hit with. Fees of £25 per late payment are typical, spending over your limit will also get you hit with a fee of £20 or £30, and there may even be an annual fee for just having the card. If you do have a card with an annual fee, ditch it straight away for one without – there are plenty to choose from, see e.g. **moneysupermarket.com**.

Interest charges on larger balances

The interest charged on a £99 purchase doesn't look too good, but see what happens if you have a balance of, for example, £3,000 – this has been the average credit card balance in the UK over the last few years. (We have the highest average credit card balance figure in Europe by the way.)

Check out a minimum repayment calculator on, for example, **thisismoney.co.uk**, to work out how much you could save on your credit card balance by paying just a little more each month. If you paid off only 2% of an average £3,000 balance (i.e. £60) each month, it would take you forty-five years and cost an extra £7,600 in interest to pay it off! If your credit card company let you pay a minimum of only 1% off per month (store cards often do this), it would take you over 100 years to pay off this debt! But if you made a fixed payment of say £100 per month, it would take you only three and a quarter years to pay it off, at an interest cost of £1,000.

Transfer your balance instead

Check out credit card comparison sites, such as **money.co.uk** or **moneysupermarket.com** for the best deals on balance transfers for credit cards. You can get credit cards that offer 0% interest rates on balances transferred to them for up to eighteen months. You transfer your credit card debt to this card and pay off as much as you can afford as a fixed amount each month and all this money goes to pay off the actual amount you owe rather than any interest.

Look out for cards that have the lowest one-off fee, usually between 2 and 3%, i.e. a fee of £60–90 for a £3,000 balance transferred. But you have to not make new spendings on your transfer card or a lot of the benefit is lost.

Transfer your balance again

If you can pay off your balance before the end of the 0% free period, brilliant. If not, then apply for a different card to transfer the balance to for another free period. Don't just stick with the new card, as when the special rate ends, the interest rate will usually jack up to near the 20% mark.

In general, balance transfers work well if you are likely to pay off the whole amount in around three years. More than that and the fees mean that you are better off getting a cheap loan.

Cut the interest rate without changing cards

Just ask your credit card company for a better interest rate. It sounds simple because it is. If you have another card with a lower rate, mention that and ask if they can match it. Otherwise point to deals you have seen and ask if they can match them. If you can't get all your credit card debt interest down to your lowest rate this way, then ask if you can transfer some balance to the card you have which is charging you the lowest interest, and ask if the lower rate will continue for the lifetime of the debt.

Cheap loans

If you have credit card debt which you can't foresee paying off within one or two years and you can't balance transfer, you are much, **much** better off getting a cheap loan, maybe even from the same credit card company.

Uk.zopa.com is a great service that links individual borrowers and lenders to agree terms for a loan. You can get a good deal here, and it has the advantage of cutting the banks out of the deal. Otherwise many credit card companies offer the next best loans with their balance transfer deals for the life of the loan – you can get an interest rate with these of 6–8%, which is often better than you can get with your bank. Talk to your credit card company about this, and look at e.g. **moneysupermarket.com** to find out other balance transfer deals.

The way to get the lowest interest payments of all is as secured lending on a property, i.e. a mortgage. If you already have a mortgage, you can talk to your mortgage provider about increasing your borrowing – but beware you then need to increase your regular payments in line with this new borrowing, otherwise you will pay even more interest because mortgages are designed to last for many years. Do be aware that you may lose your home if you don't keep up repayments.

Best credit cards for cashback

Getting cashback on credit card payments is a great idea – as long as the plastic doesn't tempt you to buy more than you should, and as long as you can manage your money well enough to be able to pay off the balance in full every month, of course. And don't transfer balances to a cashback card – the temptation to spend and so not reduce the debt is too strong.

So, health warning over, you can get cashback deals which give you money back on all of your purchases, e.g. a 1% cashback deal means you earn 1p cashback for every £1 you spend. So if you spend £1,000 a month on your cashback card by the end of the year you earn £120. American Express often offer the best deals – up to 1.25% cashback – but the Halifax and the Co-op also offer a good 1% rate.

Many of the cards offer rewards rather than actual cashback, so choose one that is suitable for you. For example, the John Lewis Partnership card offers 1% cashback on purchases made in John Lewis or **ocado.com**, but 0.5% cashback on purchases everywhere else. Some cards offer higher cashback rates but an annual fee – not good for you if your use of the card could be minimal sometimes, e.g. if you had to belt-tighten. Check a comparison site, e.g. **moneysavingexpert.com**, for current deals.

Insurance protection

Don't sign up for the credit card or a loan company's payment protection insurance, and ask to stop cover if you already have it with a credit card. Often this insurance is invalid for your circumstances (e.g. the employment section doesn't cover you if you're self-employed, and you aren't covered for redundancy if your job is under threat), and if you do want it there are much cheaper ways of getting it than through your credit card.

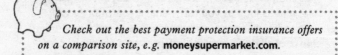

Check out the best payment protection insurance offers on a comparison site, e.g. **moneysupermarket.com**.

Reclaim payment protection insurance

If you have been mis-sold payment protection insurance (e.g. the box was automatically ticked for you, or you were told it was compulsory [which it isn't] or it wasn't suitable for your situation) you can claim it back with interest added on too, as many, many people have successfully done. Don't look for the numerous companies advertising on the Internet to get your money back for you, as they will then keep some of it for themselves. Instead contact the Financial Ombudsman for free.

MANAGING DEBT IF IT ALL GOES PEAR-SHAPED

Don't bury your head in the sand – like a water leak, the problem isn't going to go away but instead it'll just get worse. So first you have to face where you are, and then you can seek help, and there's lots of it.

Credit card debt

1. Try to transfer your balance to a zero-interest card (see page 99) to give you time to start getting the debt down.
2. Try and claim back any charges you might have been hit with for going over your credit limit, or for late payments – these high charges (often up to £35 a shot) have been ruled as unfair by the OFT. You can try to claim back the last six years of charges. You don't need to have kept your statements in order to do this – you can request them from the credit card company (they may charge you £10 so think first if you are likely to have been hit with these charges).

The OFT ruled in June 2006 that charges above £12 were unfair so you can definitely claim for the difference if your company charged more than this, but start by asking for all the charges back. The credit card companies don't want more bad publicity on this, so they often pay up. Put all the details down in a letter and calmly ask for the total of the charges to be refunded.

You can add in interest too (a court would grant you 8% if you won the case) from the date of each charge. They are unlikely to pay the interest but it is a good bargaining tactic. **Moneysavingexpert.com** has a 'court interest calculator' if you want to try the interest rouse.

If you get nothing or hear nothing from the credit card company, take your case up with the Financial Ombudsman – this is free, whereas going to the small claims court costs.

Create a payment plan

If you can't get a zero-interest balance transfer deal, or can't keep switching between them, talk to your credit card company and ask them to reduce their interest rate. You can ask them to match another deal you have or a deal you've seen, but the key here is to try to agree between you a plan for monthly payments that you can afford that will actually pay off the debt in a reasonable period of time. Use an online 'interest on credit card debt' calculator to work out how long the debt would be paid off with differing levels of interest, and haggle with the company to give you a low enough rate which means you would actually pay off the debt sometime before you die.

Get free impartial help

If you're in debt crisis – i.e. the debts are increasing and you see no way to decrease them – there are lots of free impartial agencies that can help you:

👎 **Don't** talk to your bank first, or 'debt consolidation' agencies, or 'debt management' companies, payday lenders or loan sharks. These guys are all out to make more money out of your crisis

👍 **Do** talk to the Consumer Credit Counselling Service (**cccs.co.uk**, 0800 138 1111), or the Citizens' Advice Bureau (you can go into your local one or go to **citizensadvice.org.uk**), or **nationaldebtline.co.uk** (0808 808 4000), or the Money Advice Trust (**moneyadvicetrust.org**), or **Payplan.com** (0800 280 2816)

> *Beware similar name pretenders – the associations listed above are the official debt advice centres, which you can be sure won't be charging you a penny for their really useful help.*

No debt is so bad it can't be solved

However bad it is. In the worst-case scenario, you can declare yourself bankrupt – many successful business people do this and come back to make another million. The debt advice agencies can advise you for free as to what is best for your situation. In most circumstances this will likely start with:

👍 A plan to prevent any new borrowing

👍 A plan to organize your repayments so that you are paying off the highest interest rates first

👍 A plan to reduce the interest rates you are paying. The agencies can even contact lenders for you and help to get rates reduced

SUMMARY

Do use a credit card to help you bridge the gap between when payday comes and when you need to pay for things, and use a cashback credit card to give you money back when you spend. But beware the evils of credit cards. If you can, always pay off the balance in full as you will save yourself £££s. If you can't, then be proactive – speak to the credit card companies and agree a plan where you can reduce the interest rate and will be able to pay off the debt in a reasonable time. Government-sponsored debt agencies are free to use and are there to help if things get tough.

12. Holidays on the Cheap

'TRAVEL BROADENS THE MIND AND EMPTIES THE WALLET.'

STAYCATION

Staying UK *saves* the day

Beware the hidden costs of foreign travel:

- 👍 Transfers from airports
- 👍 Buying food at airports
- 👍 Insurance
- 👍 Buying special equipment
- 👍 Buying gifts and foreign knick-knacks etc.

If you holiday in the UK, you know what you are getting and how much it will cost to get there, and also you are not so tempted to splash out while you are away.

Camping and caravanning are great cheap ways to holiday in the UK – see **camp-sites.co.uk** for a full searchable list of campsites and their facilities in the UK, and **ukparks.com** for a listing of caravan sites. Look particularly at the ones which have won the David Bellamy Conservation Award scheme. Or for super cheap camping try **campinmygarden.com**.

To hire camper vans, check out **wickedcampers.co.uk** who do special offers especially on short breaks, and also look at **motorholme.co.uk** (the extra 'l' is correct) for the biggest selection of locations to hire camper vans from, and drop them back to, in Europe.

Do consider the cost, both in green and in pound terms, of the fuel you will use driving a large petrol-hungry vehicle around.

If you want a little more luxury than camping, yet still with the full nature experience, then glamorous camping – Glamping – may be for you. Look into Feather Down Farm Days, **featherdown.co.uk** – twenty-five beautiful farm locations across the country dotted with tents filled with real furniture, real beds and real plumbing. Also check out **ukcampsite.co.uk** for a list of good glamping sites.

Yurt tents are another similar option, see **goglamping.net** for worldwide glamping, **yurtworks.co.uk** in Cornwall, **hiddenvalleyyurts.co.uk** and **theyurtfarm.co.uk** for the Welsh experience, and **woodlandtipis.co.uk** in Herefordshire, or **lake-district-yurts.co.uk** for a fabulous place to stay in the Lakes for a fraction of the usual cost.

Home from home

If you do want to stay in a house, you don't need to rent somewhere expensive to get a great place to stay – you can home exchange instead. The biggest site for home exchanging with the most properties worldwide is **homeexchange.com**. It's American run, so has the most properties in the USA, but also has the largest number of members of any of the home exchange sites.

Annual membership is $120, but you can pay for just a month at a time if you want to try it out (be sure to cancel payments ongoing as they are automatically renewed). The membership fee is all you pay – contacting other members, viewing property details and arranging to swap is all absolutely free.

Smaller sites are cheaper to join. Good sites are **ukholidayswapshop.co.uk** *(currently £20 per year) and* **guardianhomeexchange.co.uk** *(£35 per year).*

TIPS FOR SUCCESSFUL HOME EXCHANGING:

- The biggest issue is trusting your home to strangers. So to put your mind at rest, check the people you are contacting are real people (e.g. ask what their jobs are and google them, or check them on Facebook). If you have a spare room or cupboard that you can put precious things in, whether valuable or breakable, then fit a lock to the door if there isn't currently one

- Be honest about your home – max up its good points, but don't go overboard. Chances are visitors won't be spending that much of the day in your house as they will most likely be touring local attractions, so they may not mind that your kitchen isn't architect designed, unless you said it was

- Location is all – there are good points about every location so make sure you bring them out. People want to visit cities as well as chocolate box villages

House-sit

You can stay in a nice house for free if you're good with pets and responsible enough to be a house-sitter. You can find house-sitting posts on websites such as **gumtree.com**, but if you can be available for frequent placements you will even get paid a small wage for house-sitting if you get accepted by a house-sitting agency – check out **homesitters.co.uk**, or **housesitters.co.uk**.

Another option is to be a live-in guardian of an empty property and pay about 50% of the usual rent for that property – look at **liveinguardians.com**. You have to be over twenty-one years old with references and the lets are often short term.

Stay for free in a bothy – a remote, and very basic, building, often situated in some of the most beautiful parts of the countryside. See **mountainbothies.org.uk**.

Return to university

Bask in the hallowed halls of Oxford and Cambridge by taking advantage of their holiday room rental schemes. The accommodation might be basic, but it's cheap and will be situated right in the heart of the city. See **universityrooms.co.uk** for more information.

VENTURING ABROAD

Working holidays

It's easier than ever to work your way around the world and many people have done it – James Taris is one such person and you can find out how to emulate his free travel exploits on his website **travelwithoutmoney.com**. Local exchange trading schemes (LETS) are the foundation of how it works and a typical example is that you stay on a farm for free and pick fruit for a few hours each day.

The best way to travel this way is just to start, and keep all social media mechanisms tweeting and facebooking away and see where you can get to next.

Bartering techniques

For any world travelling, bear in mind the power of barter – packets of Marlboro cigarettes and bottles of whisky (heavier but more valuable) are almost global currency. They can help with many a negotiation and, if necessary, get you out of a tight spot. It's also great when travelling in developing countries to bring children's books with you, pens or crayons – these small gifts can go a long way in helping you to make friends and travel easily. Also bring photos of your family and friends to show and share.

Volunteering holidays

For more organized working holidays, look into the possibilities of working in the UK and abroad on conservation holidays with the National Trust or the National Trust for Scotland (the latter runs 'thistle camps', see **nts.org.uk**), or the British Trust for Conservation Volunteers (**bctv.org.uk**) who offer volunteering abroad as well. For longer term foreign volunteering, look into the VSO, **vso.org.uk**, and **worldwidevolunteering.org.uk**.

Guidebooks

As a former guidebook writer I hate to say it, but it's rare that you need to buy a guidebook any more. Free mini city guidebooks are available from a variety of websites, e.g. the Lloyds TSB website, **lloydstsb.com**. For the rest of your travel information needs, if you plan in advance you can print off most of the information you need from the Internet beforehand, and if you have a smartphone you can have access to worldwide maps.

If you do want a guidebook, first look in your local charity shop, as there is no need for a totally up-to-date book (especially for historical ruins), and then check **abebooks.com** for very cheap second-hand books.

ACCOMMODATION

Holiday beds on the cheap

Why pay silly money to stay in a hotel when you can rent someone's spare room for little, or bring your sleeping bag and crash on their sofa for less, or swap your sofa for theirs for nothing? This way you will also get to 'meet the locals', whether they are in Newcastle or New York, and so can get inside tips on getting the most out of an area. Check out **crashpadder.com**, **airbnb.com**, **couchsurfing.org** and **spare-room.co.uk**.

You can choose accommodation in places you want to go to, or you can also do the reverse – feed in a suggested trip to the websites – location and dates if possible – and have people with pads to crash at or couches to surf on suggest their places to stay to you, with accompanying itinerary ideas.

Most of these websites require you to pay an amount upfront (couch surfing is the exception as it's not for profit) and you are charged cancellation fees for late cancellation, so be sure you want to stay before booking.

> *Many of the homeowners on **spare-room.co.uk** are up for trading work for a free night's stay – cleaning and babysitting are both popular options.*

YHA

For more formalized cheap holiday beds, remember the YHA is not only for youths – **yha.org.uk** has thousands of beds across the UK from £6 for a bed in a barn. You don't have to join but if you do join then the temporary membership fee of £3 per night is waived (standard membership fee is £16 per year). For London, **travelstay.com** finds the cheapest hostel beds the city can offer.

Bargain hotels

Travel lodges, **travelodge.co.uk**, offer reasonable travel accommodation from £19 a room. A good alternative is the Accor chain, **accorhotels.com**, which spreads across the UK, Europe and beyond offering a great range of room prices and standards. Within the Accor chain, check out **hotelformule1.com** which offer very good priced hotel rooms across the world, and an extra 10% discount for booking more than 30 days in advance.

Hotel and travel deals

👍 Many travel operators offer cheap tie-in deals with hotels – check the deal your airline shows and the deal that a travel broker, such as **expedia.com**, offers

👍 If you're travelling by train you may get a special deal on a hotel at the destination – **thetrainline.com** has deals with hotels and you can access the best price for a hotel through their website, e.g. Generator London hotel in WC1 with a single room for £14

👍 Also check out hotel comparison websites, such as **trivago.com**, which compares the prices at thousands of hotels around the world

👍 **Lastminute.com** offers great deals at 'top secret hotels', i.e. you choose the location but they only tell you exactly which hotel you will stay at just before you go

Hotel discounts

If you book directly with a hotel, always ask the receptionist if they can offer you a better price than the first quoted price. Ask if they can do a price with the add-ons removed, e.g. they might do a cheaper price without breakfast – useful if you are planning a lazy holiday and would sleep through breakfast anyway.

CHEAP INSURANCE

Reduce the cost of travel insurance

Yearly policies, for example from **insureandgo.com**, are good value if you make two or more trips a year. Direct Line offer online discounts for yearly policies. Check out an insurance comparison website to find the cheapest options, e.g. **moneysupermarket.com**.

Consider how much cover you actually need and whether you might already have an insurance policy which covers you. For example, if you have life cover you don't need your travel policy to cover your life, or if you have home insurance which covers possessions even when out of the home and abroad (as some do) then you don't need travel insurance to cover those either.

Medical holiday insurance for free

If you're travelling in Europe then you'll be entitled to free or reduced cost state medical treatment if you carry the European Travel Insurance Card, which replaces the old E111 form. You can obtain cards from the Post Office, they cost £2 and last for three years.

Don't accidentally buy insurance

Many companies, from rental cottages to airlines, package holidays to even concert bookings, will automatically sign you up for buying their travel insurance unless you *actively* opt out. Be active – uncheck the box.

HOLIDAY MONEY

Travel money – use your card abroad

Using your debit cards abroad **is** cheaper than buying foreign currency in the UK. There are a lot of myths surrounding the perils of using your bank debit card abroad. Yes, your bank will charge you for using your card abroad, whether in ATMs, or in shops/restaurants etc., but the money you have to pay on the charges and commissions you more than save by getting a better exchange rate. It works like this:

👍 When you change sterling for currency while in the UK, e.g. at your bank or the post office, you change at the 'sell' rate (because they are selling you euros)

👍 When you use your card abroad you exchange at the 'buy' rate

👍 The difference between these two rates makes all the difference

👍 So, if you buy 200 Euros at the very best rate available in the UK, it would currently cost you £169

👍 And if you spend 200 Euros while abroad on your debit card it would cost you (even after the average charge) £155, and on average £160 to take 200 Euros out from an ATM abroad (again after the average charge made by your bank)

But do be aware that the charges levied by banks on their debit cards vary, e.g. NatWest charges £1.25 for each transaction abroad in a shop or restaurant, while HSBC charges £1.75 a pop, whereas Metro bank and the Halifax clarity card charge nothing. So check out what your bank charges and consider changing accounts if you go abroad often. And do be aware that many credit cards levy much higher fees than banks' debit cards.

When paying for things abroad with a debit or credit card, always pay in the local currency to get the best exchange rate, not in sterling.

Tell your bank before you travel where you intend to go so they don't identify your overseas transactions as possibly fraudulent and block your card.

Buying travel money

It's a good idea to take some currency with you in case your destination airport doesn't have an ATM. Don't just turn up at the airport and buy currency – this will get you the worst deal of all.

Print off a voucher from Iceplc's website and you will get the UK's best exchange rates for euros for collection at certain London branches.

Check a site such as **moneysupermarket.com** to find the best exchange deals after charges. Beware those that require ordering online because you will have to pay with a card, and the purchase of currency with a card will be treated by your bank as a foreign exchange transaction, which means they'll hit you with charges. This means that a lot of the online currency deals with free delivery or collection, which seem good options, rarely are. Instead, opt for the best deal on the day for pre-ordering with a regular bank/bureau or post office, where you can pay in person in cash.

Your own bank may well not offer the best deal so do look around.

> • *Never pay for currency with a credit card as you will instantly be hit with daily interest charges. (You will pay a fee for paying by debit card but no extra interest charges.)*
> • *Exchanging for cash will give you a better rate than exchanging for travellers' cheques.*

Pre-paid cards

Pre-paid cards are a good way to stick to a budget when abroad. They are also a way of having the convenience of a card for payments if you don't have a bank account or have a poor credit record. FairFX charges no fee for a shop/ restaurant transaction, but you get worse exchange rates using them than using a bank's debit card, and every pre-paid card charges you for each ATM withdrawal.

SUMMARY

From camping to glamping, home exchanging and couch surfing, to volunteering or working holidays – there are hundreds of ways to have a great holiday without great expense. Bargain with hotels, and compare prices to find the cheapest travel insurance and you can save £££s. Then get the best deal on holiday money and you have a recipe for a fantastic holiday.

13. Saving on Your Holiday Travel

FLIGHTS

Cheapest flights and package holidays

There are a huge number of companies promising to offer you the cheapest of cheap flights and holidays abroad. How do you work out which to use? The answer is that there are a few different types of offers so it depends what kind of trip you are planning.

Be flexible and find the cheapest flights ever

The budget airlines often advertise sales of £1 or even 1p flights. One approach for getting a cheap holiday abroad is to decide to go to wherever you can get a very cheap flight for. You can look direct on the budget airlines' sites or you can use the flightchecker tool on **moneysavingexpert.com** to find the very cheapest flights for a particular destination in a particular time frame. Or use the tool to select the option of travelling anywhere and set a minimum price, e.g. finding you all flights below £10.

If you know where and when you want to go

The Internet has a huge number of 'screenscrapers' to find you cheap flights. These companies check the prices of hundreds of different airlines and online travel agents to hundreds of destinations and 'scrape' the prices off their screens and display them to you. These can be excellent ways of finding cheap flights.

Some of the best screenscrapers are **momondo.com**, **moneysupermarket.com** (which includes some charter airlines), **skyscanner.net** (which includes some low-cost airlines), and **kayak.co.uk**, which has options such as multi destinations.

Online travel agents

After you have looked at the screenscrapers, you should also check online travel agents, such as **travelocity.com**, **expedia.com**, **opodo.com**, **ebookers.com**, **budgetlonghaul.com** and **netflights.com**. Flight brokers such as these have commercial relations with airlines and so can offer their own special deals. They also offer discounts on hotels if you book flights with them. Their deals vary so check a few.

Another one to look for is **priceline.co.uk**. With this site you bid a price for a ticket, which can save you money if you are flexible about when you fly.

*Look at **low-cost-airline-guide.com** to find out which budget airlines, such as Ryanair, Easyjet etc., fly to where you want to go.*

Package holidays

For traditional package holidays look at charter planes: **moneysupermarket.com** shows unused seats on charter planes and so can often have the best priced tickets for popular routes. Other cheap holiday options to try are Thomas Cook, Thomsons, Monarch airlines and **lowcostholidays.com**.

Check if there is a special deal with your credit or debit card

Sometimes credit and debit cards operate special deals with particular airlines, e.g. currently Visa Signature cardholders get 15% off all flights with Southwest Airlines. Check with your provider to see if there are any current offers.

Beat back the extras that budget airlines charge

The budget airlines have a huge number of hidden extra charges – if you know them, you can beat them:

- Always book and check-in online for the cheapest fares and reduced admin charges. Even if you're at the airport – find an Internet café and book there, even paying to print out your boarding card, it saves you £s compared to walking over to the airline desk and booking there. Crazy but true

- Pay with a Mastercard prepaid debit card for Ryanair flights and you don't have to pay their admin handling fee (£6 for all other ways of paying). Easyjet and others such as Bmibaby and BMI use the same deal for Visa Electron payments but all other ways of paying incur nearly a £5 charge. The charges can be even higher if you pay with a credit card

👍 Be sure to uncheck boxes when booking – some airlines automatically select you to pay for extras, such as speedy boarding

👍 Take full advantage of the 10kg free hand luggage allowance rather than having to pay to stow luggage (this can cost up to £40 per bag if you book online, and £80 per bag for booking through the call centre or at the airport)

Airline credit cards

Some airlines, such as BMI and Flybe, offer a credit card deal, where if you sign up for their credit card and make a payment on it (it can be a 10p sweet) when you fly, you get a free return flight. But you still have to pay taxes, you have uncertainty over your flight time and to avoid paying interest on any payments, you have to ensure that you pay off the full balance. So it's quite a lot of hassle and you may be better off just getting yourself the cheapest flights you can.

The cheapest way to park your car to fly

Always book as early as you can to park your car at the airport; even if you book just before setting off you'll get a better price than if you just turn up. If you're travelling with an operator they may offer you a discount for a parking space at the airport, so check. Otherwise use the airport parking price comparison sites and compare with the prices offered by the airports themselves – occasionally they have special offers and are the best options, e.g. look at **airport-parking.co.uk**, **aph.com**, **skyparksecure.com** (which currently offers 11% off if you book through **moneysavingexpert.com**), **fhr-net.co.uk** (which likewise

offers 10% off if you book through the link on
moneysavingexpert.com), and also check the airport
operators themselves, **baa.com** and **parkbcp.co.uk**.

For a better deal than at any airport car parks, find a
local parking space on someone's drive – check out
parkatmyhouse.co.uk, and **parkonmydrive.com**. You can
then take a short taxi ride to the airport costing a few
pounds, to save yourself ££s. For instance, Heathrow 'drive
up and park' prices are £17 per day whereas you can rent out
someone's drive nearby for £35 per week.

CAR HIRE

Car hire on the cheap

Check out the many global and local peer-to-peer car hire and
lift-sharing schemes (see Travel: Cars, Bikes and Trains, page
145) first off to see if you can get yourself a car for less.
Failing this, **moneysupermarket.com** or other comparison
sites will show you the best deals for where you're going.
Also check out tied deals with your airline or hotel, e.g. on
expedia.com.

It usually pays to book the car in advance, getting you
cheaper deals than if you just turn up at an airport and hope
for the best. When you book in advance, always be sure to
ask for add-ons at that stage and not on arrival – for
example, if you need extra drivers to be on the insurance
policy this will often cost less if pre-ordered. The same goes
for child seats for the car.

SUMMARY

Use screenscrapers and price comparison sites to get the best deals on flights, and then use the tricks of the trade to avoid the add-on charges that seem compulsory but aren't always. Avoid the airport car park and park on a nearby driveway to save ££s.

14. Buying Your Home

BIG SAVINGS ON A BIG PURCHASE

House buying

Your home is the most expensive purchase you will ever make, and a tiny percentage saving can equal big money. So it's worth thinking how to cut costs in every way. You can save £££££s.

Buying at auction

Properties sell at auction far more cheaply than through regular high street estate agents. If you buy a repossessed property or a distressed sale (e.g. after a divorce) you can get a 20 or even 30% markdown on the true price because the seller wants or needs a quick sale. But you will have to know your way around the auction process, do a lot of homework on vetting the property (with a solicitor and builder), and be prepared for potentially major refurbishment. Be sure to get clues to the property's value, e.g. using websites such as **nethouseprices.com** or **houseprices.co.uk** to find comparable prices, or a tool on **zoopla.co.uk** which values a house.

Check out a guide to buying at auction, e.g. on **primelocation.com** or **uknetguide.co.uk**. If you're still keen, check out the properties for auction at the leading auction houses: Essential Information Group (**eigroup.co.uk**), Allsop (**allsop.co.uk**), the Property Auctions People (**auctionpropertyforsale.co.uk**), Savills (**savills.co.uk**) and **whitehotproperty.com**.

The easiest way to get auction prices is where an estate agent handles the selling, even though it is an auctioned property – this is the case for properties on the site **propertyearth.net**, and you can also find auctioned properties handled by estate agents in the back of local papers, and by contacting estate agents directly and asking them if they have any auction property.

Buy and build

You can make great savings by buying a wreck and rebuilding, or by buying land and building a home on it – it will typically cost around 20–40% less than the equivalent home already built. But there is a great danger of going over budget, and of going through hell. A good way to keep costs down if you self-build is by buying a pre-built timber frame, e.g. from a good value supplier such as Scot Frame, **scotframe.co.uk**, or another Scottish firm, **deesidetimberframe.com**. These can cost as little as £15,000 for a house, and take around £4,000 to put up over a few days.

Working out how much the rest of the build including fixtures and fittings should cost is as easy as finding out how long a piece of string is, but a very rough estimate would be £40 per square foot for build cost, working out to around £120,000 for a three-bedroom house.

If you do opt to self-build, tying builders to an all-in quote is difficult but worth achieving, and be sure never to take the first quote. Look around for advice before starting anything, e.g. on Internet forums such as **greenbuildingforum.co.uk**. Be aware that you will of course need planning permission to build on land – look at the Government's **planningportal.gov.uk** for advice on all things planning.

> *One saving you definitely make by self-building is on stamp duty – you pay none for purchasing land – check out the **uklanddirectory.org.uk** for available land sites.*

Tricks to reduce the cost of property buying

👍 Ex-council properties sell for 10–20% less than the equivalent property that has never been council owned

👍 Flats above shops or restaurants also sell at a discount

👍 If you're buying a property around the different stamp duty thresholds (i.e. £125,000, £250,000, £500,000 and £1 million), you can keep below the threshold by paying the sellers directly for the fixtures and fittings that would otherwise be included. Be aware that you shouldn't try this for large amounts or you will have the taxman, or woman, onto you

👍 In almost any property purchase you will have much better bargaining power if you're chain free

👍 Choose a solicitor who offers you a fixed price for your conveyancing. The cheapest way to get conveyancing is through an online firm, and this can save you £££s. You can get an instant very well priced quote by just putting in the purchase price of the property at **conveyancing-warehouse.com**, or look at **onlineconveyancing.co.uk**. These and other online sites can be good if the purchase is simple and if it's not important that it's quick. If you need speed, then a regular solicitor can be better, and often the solicitor the estate agent recommends can get the job done fastest. But always get more than one quote and if the solicitor the estate agent suggests is more expensive, tell them so and they may reduce their price

👍 Get the best deal on mortgages and insurance – see the Money: Saving for Your Home chapter

Haggle with *everyone*

👍 Haggle over the price of the property by all means, especially if the market is not so buoyant and it is not your dreamiest of dream houses ever

👍 Haggle with the sellers over the cost of fixtures and fittings

👍 Haggle if the survey points out problems. If the survey uncovers changes without proof of the necessary building regulations required to make those changes, then insist the sellers buy indemnity insurance to protect you from the risk of being called to account by the local council and possibly forced to put back the changes. If you are selling and you have made such changes to the property, or notice that others were made previously, you should buy indemnity insurance to protect your buyers. This makes the sale much easier and can prevent successful haggling by the buyer

👍 Haggle with estate agents about their fee if you are renting or selling. Fees between estate agents vary enormously with no corresponding difference in service. Sometimes an estate agent will run a special offer of low fees in order to gain customers

Tricks to increase the price of your property when selling

👍 Have a major clear out before you have any agents round

👍 De-personalize – take photos down etc. Every agent will tell you the more easily people can see your house as their home, the more they will pay for it

👍 Get the windows cleaned, sweep the path and re-plant window boxes and hanging baskets, and see the £ signs in the agent's eyes

SUMMARY

There are many ways to cut down on the cost of your biggest purchase. You can save a fortune if you buy a property at auction, or if you buy land and build your property on it. For those of us who aren't quite so daring and are instead trying to make our way up the regular housing ladder, make sure you haggle – with the seller, the estate agent, the builder. And agreeing a fixed price wherever possible can save you heaps of heartache and thousands of pounds.

15. Home Improvements

SAVE MONEY WHEN DOING UP YOUR HOME

Home and energy grants

There are many different grants for all sorts of aspects of doing up your home – make sure you apply for what you might be eligible for. Start by searching the grants database on the government's Energy Saving Trust website – **energysavingtrust.org.uk**. You can also contact Enact Energy, **enactenergy.co.uk**, to find out if you may be eligible for grants for a new boiler or for home insulation, which saves £££s every year on heating bills. If you are over seventy, you are automatically eligible, also if you receive certain benefits.

Installing solar panels is a great way to reduce your energy bills and get paid extra on top – see Monthly Utility Bills (page 28).

Making money from what you move on

Try to sell or recycle everything you are replacing in your home:

👍 A friend made £600 by selling an old water tank, which their builder had so very kindly offered to take away for them. Look at **yell.com** or **kellysearch.co.uk** to find local scrap metal merchants and compare prices

👍 If you have any strange antique items that an antique shop wouldn't be interested in, such as a copper bath or Edwardian horse box, try salvage companies, e.g. **Lassco.co.uk** is the UK's biggest architectural salvage company, and they buy and sell

👍 You can also sell plastics, for example to **ckpolymers.co.uk**, or **apr-ltd.co.uk**

👍 Try to freecycle other unwanted goods which would sell for very little

👍 Re-use items yourself – check out **recyclethis.co.uk** for hundreds of ideas of how to re-use or recycle practically everything

👍 In the final scenario when something cannot be re-sold or given away or re-used by yourself, check out **ReduceReuseRecycle.co.uk** for locations of where practically everything can be recycled or donated to a local scrap store, which re-uses items for arts and crafts

Buying recycled

When you're re-fitting your house, you'll be amazed at the products you can buy which have previously had a life as something else – e.g. kitchen surfaces made from old plastic bottles etc. Look at s**mile-plastics.co.uk** or **thegreenhaus.co.uk** for ideas on recycled objects of beauty.

Check out Nigel's Eco Store, **nigelsecostore.com,** *and* **love-eco.co.uk** *for environmentally sustainable useful house gadgets and equipment.*

Always be de-cluttering

Before you refurb or refit, find out what you actually have in the first place – de-clutter and you might discover some old wallpaper, or paint, or chairs, or goodness knows what that are actually just the job.

Anything you don't need or want anymore sell on eBay, antique shops, or similar, or give away on freecycle or similar. Often if you are thinking of giving a room a new lease of life with re-decoration, you can achieve a lot of the freshening up you were looking for by simple de-cluttering.

Choosing builders

For any major work get a couple of builders to quote for the work, and tell them that you will be securing multiple quotes, to encourage them to come up with a competitive quote first time around. Make sure builders quote an all-in price for the work, not a quote based on their time. To find good workmen ask around neighbours, friends and people you actually know on social media sites. Beware

Worth looking at is **ratedpeople.co.uk** *– you can find builders, plumbers, painters etc. here whom people have employed and then rated.*

recommendations on social media sites from people you don't know as these can be only as reliable as adverts.

Managing builders

👍 Ply them with tea and biscuits at regular intervals through the day so that they will want to do a better job for you

👍 Tell them what time you would like them to come, e.g. nine until five – don't let them tell you what time they are coming or they may arrive at 6 a.m.

👍 If your house is lived in while they are doing the work, ask them to do any cutting etc. outside, providing you have easy access

👍 Ask them if they have any old materials, or materials they've removed from other people's houses, which they could use in your home. They won't necessarily volunteer this information, thinking you might not want these, but they can be happy to give them to you if you ask. Our shower room floor and worktop came to us for free this way

Discounts at building shops

Always buy from trade shops whenever possible. You don't need to be a trade professional to buy from most of the trade shops for plumbing, timber, paints etc. If a trade shop does only want to buy from a registered person, ask your builder to buy for you. You can apply for the Buildstore trade card, see **buildstore.co.uk**, by showing interest in doing a self-build. You then get discounts on numerous trade and non-trade shops, such as Build Centre, Plumb Centre and Carpetright.

And here are some other discounts to be aware of:

- 👍 If you're over sixty, you qualify for a 10% off card from every B&Q every Wednesday

- 👍 Homebase is part of the Nectar group

- 👍 The Ikea family store card gives you 25% off the whole family range of furniture, plus free insurance against damages during home delivery, and a free cup of tea or coffee from the store's cafe midweek

Home decoration for free

Register to be on a TV programme on re-decoration, e.g. *DIY SOS*, through **beonashow.com**. You get a load of work done on your house for free, and the teams usually leave behind heaps of high-quality quick-drying paints and other materials.

Fabrics for less

The curtain factory outlet (**curtainfactoryoutlet.co.uk**) is a huge London warehouse stocking thousands of fabrics, all £6.99 a metre. Despite the name they also stock upholstery fabrics and dress fabrics. **Endoflinefabrics.co.uk** has hugely reduced remnant fabrics which it will dispatch to you. Or contact places like **fabricworldlondon.co.uk** who will come to your house with thousands of fabrics and make suggestions for a flat fee of £50.

Tiles for half the price

Chequerboard tile patterns with black (or another colour) and white for bathroom or kitchen walls make very attractive designs. They also cost half the price of tiling in any other mix of colours because plain white tiles are the very cheapest to buy, so using them in equal measures to any other colour saves ££s.

Wallpaper for free

You can create a single stand-out wall of wallpaper by creating a patchwork of wallpaper, using small free samples of wallpaper from any decoration shop or from some online wallpaper shops, e.g. **wallpaperdirect.co.uk**. Or you can simply use small cut-offs from old wallpaper rolls you or friends might have – if none, try posting a wanted ad on freecycle for old wallpaper. The quality isn't important in a patchwork and people are often glad to offload their old bits. Liberty's London shop shows how stunning this effect can be in its jewellery department.

Skip-diving

Keep an eye out for useful items in skips which the owners don't want but you might. You can get wood for shelving, old tables and chairs to do up, and other bits and bobs for free this way. Make sure you ask the owner of the skip before taking them and you'll stay on the right side of the law.

Wallpaper for children's bedrooms

Rather than re-decorating children and teenagers' bedrooms for each latest phase or craze, stick up the newest posters with wallpaper paste and simply turn them into wallpaper, any angle anywhere. When a new poster of the latest flavour of the month arrives, simply paste it over last month's idol.

Design ideas

Find architecture and design students from any architecture or design college near you and offer them lunch to come to your place and have ideas about it. We got our best ideas for design changes to our house this way.

Transforming wooden floors for very little

You can entirely transform damaged old wooden floorboards by painting them. You can use cheap emulsion paint if you varnish it with Dulux Diamond – an extremely strong product, so a little goes a very long way. Our hallway still looks superb ten years down the line after this treatment (you don't have to emulate the Jackson Pollock splatter design we created underneath ...).

Or you can sand down wooden floors by hiring a sanding machine and doing it yourself – hiring on weekdays will give you a better price than at weekends.

Creative painting

👍 There is no need to buy the expensive paint sold by shops to treat water stains on walls or ceilings – simply mix equal parts of white gloss and emulsion and the stain will be sealed and covered

👍 You can make your own paint – a search on Google will reveal many milk-based recipes (yes, really). Then to create the colour buy natural pigments from an art shop and add to the liquid. Make sure you apply the paint quickly because milk goes sour (but once it's applied, it won't smell). Apply further coats for deeper colour

👍 Easier still is to mix your own colours from odd ends of paint you have – our living room ceiling used to be a beautiful blue worthy of Farrow and Ball courtesy of this method. Top tip: leave some extra and decant to a small tin to keep it usable for touching up

👍 It's easy to make your own wood stains – make tea with strong tea leaves and allow it to steep for an hour and then apply it to wood surfaces. If the resulting colour isn't strong enough, create your own iron acetate by putting wire wool in a jam jar of vinegar overnight. Sieve the liquid the next day and apply with a brush

👍 If you have a small area to paint, buying one or two match pots can be cheaper than buying a whole pot of paint

👍 Re-paint the kitchen units for a totally new look, for a fraction of the price of a new one. If they are wood then this is straightforward (sand them down, apply primer, then colour). If they are melamine, you need to buy specialist melamine primer then apply regular paint, e.g. in eggshell finish (which is easy to apply and best for kitchen units)

Changing doorknobs on kitchen units or chests of drawers can transform them for very little.

SUMMARY

There are hundreds of ways of giving your house a major makeover without it costing an arm or a leg. A patchwork of wallpaper samples makes a great feature wall, re-painting the kitchen units creates a new look for a fraction of the price of a new kitchen, painted wooden floors can look stunning and cost very little, and why buy expensive paint when you can make your own and create unique blended colours?

16. Cleaning Your Home

IN WITH THE OLD

Cleaning the old-fashioned way

As with toiletries, cleaning products come in a range of expensive packaging and all with miracle ingredients. Yet the real miracle is how these companies continue to rake in our hard-earned pennies, when one can clean just as easily with a simple lemon.

Cue the return of more natural substances, which you can use to clean your home and its contents in the old-fashioned way. There are three cheap and natural things that do a great job of cleaning – and as an added benefit they're much less harmful to the environment and our families than shop-bought products. These wonder items are:

1. lemon
2. bicarbonate of soda (bicarb)
3. white vinegar

Lemons can be found for about 20p each, bicarbonate of soda is around £2.50 for one kilogram and white vinegar is around £3 for five litres. Using these extremely cheap and universally available items will save you ££s compared to the expensive cleaning brands found in supermarkets.

Save old tea towels, vests, or T-shirts to use as wiping or rubbing cloths so that you don't need to buy J-cloths or kitchen roll.

Cleaning with lemons

Lemons are acidic and provide some antiseptic and antibacterial properties for cleaning. Find out more at **housekeeping.about.com**.

👍 Clean the oven with lemons – fill an ovenproof dish with water and squeeze the juice of several lemons into the water. Put it into the oven and heat to medium heat. When the water boils, turn the heat down so the water simmers. Turn off the oven when almost all of the water is gone. While the oven is still hot, clean it with a damp cloth

👍 Lemons against limescale. Limescale is the biggest killer of washing machines and dishwashers, but to keep it at bay you don't need to buy the dedicated anti-limescale products. Just pour one cup of lemon juice (or white vinegar) inside the washing machine soap powder dispenser, or directly into the bottom of the dishwasher and run a normal wash without clothes or dishes

👍 To clean your electric kettle with lemons, just mix half a cup of lemon juice with a cup of water, put it in the kettle and bring to boil. Leave it overnight and then rinse out

👍 Put shower heads to soak overnight in lemon juice

👍 To clean taps with lemons, soak a cloth in lemon juice and wrap it around the tap and leave it overnight (or a cloth soaked in vinegar will do the same job)

👍 You can clean brass and copper and also make a very serviceable furniture polish by mixing one cup of olive oil with half a cup of lemon juice. Rub it into your wooden furniture or brass ornaments to get it gleaming

👍 Clear stains off your kitchen counter by leaving lemon juice on it for a few minutes

The many uses of bicarbonate of soda

Bicarbonate of soda (bicarb) is very similar to baking powder but cleans a lot better (and isn't so good for making cakes with).

👍 Make a paste of bicarb and water and use it on a cloth to clean the sink

👍 To clean your drain, pour sixteen tablespoons of bicarb down the sink and then pour down 120 millilitres of white vinegar. They will fizz when mixed up and then you can rinse through with boiling water

👍 To get rid of rust from a metal table or chair legs, make a paste of one tablespoon of bicarb with a teaspoon of water. Wipe the rust with a damp cloth, then scrub gently with a piece of aluminium foil and wipe it clean with a soft cloth

👍 Make a scouring powder by mixing bicarb with salt and use it on greasy surfaces

👍 To shine up silver, apply a paste of water and bicarb with a damp sponge, rinse it off and polish it dry

- To clean marks such as crayon, pencil or grease off walls, use bicarb on a wet sponge and scrub gently

- To get rid of pet smells and freshen your carpets, sprinkle some bicarb on the carpet, leave for ten minutes and then vacuum up

- To clean fruit or vegetable well but easily, put them in a bowl of water with a sprinkle of bicarbonate of soda, wash and then rinse

- You can give your chopping board a really deep clean by spreading bicarb over the surface and spraying with vinegar. Let it fizz for a while and then rinse it off with hot water

- You can get rid of water spots from wooden floors by putting a bicarb solution on a damp cloth and applying to the floor (remember not to get the wood too wet as this can damage it)

- A tablespoon of bicarb in a pint of water makes a great kitchen or bathroom floor-cleaning solution

- For removing tough oven grease, warm the oven and then make a paste from bicarb and a little water and rub into the burnt-on stains with a cloth that is a little wet with lemon juice or vinegar

Cleaning with white vinegar

Vinegar is an acidic liquid which is produced as a result of fermentation. It's useful in killing germs, mould and bacteria. Find out more at **vinegartips.com/cleaning** and you'll wonder how you ever managed without white vinegar!

- 👍 You can mix one-part water with one-part vinegar and spray onto surfaces. Use this in your bathroom, on the cooker, on worktops and floors

- 👍 Vinegar is a natural fabric softener: add half a cup to the rinse cycle

- 👍 Clean the microwave by mixing half a cup of water with half a cup of white vinegar in a microwavable container and then turn on the microwave for two minutes. Wipe all the surfaces clean afterwards and stains and smells will go

- 👍 Mix vinegar 50:50 with borax (a white powder available from chemists' or builders' shops) to make a thick anti-limescale paste to deep clean taps, tiles, basins and baths

- 👍 Clean dishcloths and sponges by soaking them overnight in a solution of water with a dash of vinegar

- 👍 Clean mould from grout by sponging the grout with vinegar, leaving it for a few minutes and then scrubbing off with an old toothbrush

- 👍 For a cheap loo clean, pour vinegar down the toilet, scrub it and then flush

- 👍 You can make your windows sparkle by spraying them with a mixture of water and vinegar (a cup of vinegar in a gallon of water) and polishing off

- 👍 Clean sticky scissors with a cloth soaked in undiluted vinegar

Don't use vinegar on marble as it damages the surface.

Other natural solutions

Unscented soap, without petroleum distillates, is biodegradable and can be used to clean many things, especially an iron. Rub a bar of it over a hot (switched off) iron: this will smell a bit, but after you've rubbed it off with a clean cloth, the smell will go and the iron will glide much more smoothly next time you're pressing

Use eucalyptus oil for general cleaning, removing stickers, freshening up your car and reviving stainless steel

Use very cheap borax, e.g. from Boots or Wilkinsons, to remove stains from clothes – pre-soak the clothes in water with half a cup of borax, then wash normally. 'Ecoballs' are chemical-free environmentally friendly devices which produce ionized oxygen, lifting out dirt from clothes wash after wash after wash. They also work on quick wash cycles and at low temperatures (thirty degrees) so saving you electricity and water. They cost around £10 for a set to last 150 washes, i.e. costing 7p per wash.

There are other natural substances that also make great cleaning products, have a look at **eartheasy.com/live_ nontoxic_solutions.htm** for ideas on creating non-toxic products. For instance, you can use cornstarch to clean windows, as furniture polish and to shampoo rugs and carpets.

Brilliant baby wipes

For all-purpose kitchen and bathroom quick cleans, don't overlook the supermarkets' cheapest, most basic range of baby wipes. You might want the soft ones to clean baby's little face after dinner, but the cheap and nasty ones are perfect for working on the seemingly indelible stains left on furniture and floors by that dinner. Don't use baby wipes with added aloe vera or other scents as these leave a residue on surfaces.

SUMMARY

Save the old-fashioned way by using the old-fashioned ways of cleaning – lemons, bicarb and white wine vinegar – and you'll never again need to walk down the household cleaning items aisle in the supermarket, or wonder if you need a dedicated cleaning product for the bathroom floor, or for the kitchen taps, or the furniture. Clean the traditional way and you'll save ££s every time you wash the floor or clean the oven.

17. Travel: Cars, Bikes and Trains

CAR COST-CUTTING

Car clubs

These days you don't need to buy a car to have use of a car. Car clubs are a great way of having a car for a day, or a few hours. There are many local schemes springing up around the country, **citycarclub.co.uk** has cars to rent in fourteen major UK cities from Edinburgh to Southampton, and **Streetcar.co.uk** is in nine and counting. Charges can be hourly, daily or monthly and the clubs also have vans for hire.

Or you can hire a car for a day or a week from someone who lives near you with a car sitting idle – check out **whipcar.com**.

Lift-share schemes

You may not even need to hire a car yourself to make a journey by car – check out **liftshare.com/uk** or **nationalcarshare.co.uk**, or **london.liftshare.com**, or **tactranliftshare.com** to connect with other people and see if you can share a journey together, whether it's a regular journey such as a commute, or a one-off visit somewhere. There are similar schemes to this all round the world, which are useful to check out if you are travelling. Visit **zipcar.com**, **goloco.org**.

Car sharing doesn't usually affect your insurance unless you do it for a profit, but check with your insurance provider to be sure.

Make a delivery

Planning a trip from Luton to Lancaster? Take someone's newly purchased Indian rug with you and deliver it to them to cut your costs – check out **anyvan.com**. Look at the list of items for delivery and the location details and if there is a delivery which fits in with your travel plans, then make an offer of a price for which you will do the delivery.

Check that you and your car can handle the size and weight of the item, and check if the item would need extra insurance.

Buying a car

If you do need to buy a car, a good bet for getting one cheaply with some guarantees is the car supermarkets (**car-supermarket.com** has branches all over the country, **carcraft.co.uk** is also nationwide, **cargiant.co.uk** is the oldest and biggest company, but only has a branch in London; also look at **broadspeed.com** and **oneswoop.com**).

You can save money by buying from abroad – check out **ezilon.com**, a good comparison website, or look at **carbusters.com**. But be aware that the hassle factor with a car bought abroad can be significant. For an instant quote on shipping costs look at **shipmycar.co.uk**.

Buying second-hand wisely

There are numerous websites for second-hand cars, e.g. **autotrader.co.uk**, **loot.com**, **whatcar.com**.

👍 Be sure to check out what any given car should be worth on a valuation website before you agree to any purchase, e.g. **parkers.co.uk**

👍 Be aware of the common faults you should look for on any make and model at **usedcarexpert.co.uk**. For a car purchase which is not bottom of the range, a car broker such as **broker4cars.co.uk** can save you time and possibly £££s by doing a free search for you

👍 Before you buy, check that the second-hand vehicle is legal and in one piece. For only £20.50 **hpicheck.com** or the AA will check that the vehicle has no outstanding finance (which you would be hit with if you bought it), has not been reported as stolen by the police, has not been in an unadvertised crash and isn't an insurance write-off

Buying at auction

You can buy a car at auction online or in person – check out **britishcarauctions.co.uk** and **manheim.co.uk**. Remember that there is no comeback once the sale's completed, so if you're going in person, go for a trial visit to see how things work, check your prospective car over and don't be swayed on the day by another one.

> *Be prepared to pay with cash or a debit card and hold your nerve. You may come out with a real bargain.*

Save £££s with a 'green' car

👍 Electric and hybrid cars are exempt from road tax, from most congestion charges, and you can charge up and park an electric car for free in many places across the UK

👍 Vehicles emitting less than 100 g/km of CO_2 are exempt from the congestion charge after they have been registered with Transport for London (TfL). You could save £2,650 per year if you drive into London every day

👍 Low-emission cars are 'Band A' cars and so road tax is free as well – check out the fuel consumption and CO_2 emissions of particular makes of cars on **carfueldata.direct.gov.uk**

> *See **greencarsite.co.uk** for available and upcoming electric cars, and **electriccarsite.co.uk** for details on charging points across the country and to find out about parking charges.*

Convert your car to LPG

Liquefied petroleum gas is about 40% cheaper than standard petrol, cars that run on it are exempt from congestion charges, and it is also better for the environment, producing 20% less carbon dioxide than regular petrol, and several times less of the other pollutants that cause cancer and make city air smell.

It costs around £700–£2,000 to have your car converted – so on an average car use of 15,000 miles a year the conversion pays for itself after eight months. And from then on you save 40% of the cost of regular petrol every time you fill up.

*Check out **lpgconversionsltd.co.uk** to talk converting. Then use **lpgmap.co.uk** to see all the stations with LPG in the country. But if you find you're nowhere near an LPG station when out and about, your car can still run on regular petrol.*

As cheap as chips

If you have an older diesel vehicle, then you could consider mixing the diesel with used vegetable oil/chip fat. (Warning: it will make a kind of barbecue smell from the exhaust!) You can have a kit fitted through **dieselveg.com** (based in Wolverhampton) and you can transfer the kit from vehicle to vehicle. It costs around £1,350 to have the mechanism fitted, but then you can save thousands of pounds on fuel over the years. If you have an older diesel vehicle and – crucially – can find a free or very cheap supply of used vegetable oil, then this is a great idea.

Generally diesel engines will use less fuel than petrol engines, but at present diesel costs more per litre than petrol.

Fuel efficiency

The fuel efficiency of your car is the main thing, whatever it runs on. The Environmental Transport Association (ETA) has a calculator on its website which gives you an idea of the costs of running a vehicle using petrol, diesel, bio diesel, electric batteries or fuel cells – check out **eta.co.uk/car_cost_ calculator**.

By filling up your car at night you can save a tiny amount as the pumps are calibrated by volume and the petrol contracts at night when it is colder.

Rescue me

Moneysupermarket.com has a good comparison tool for rescue services, but check that you don't already have this covered, for instance via your bank account benefits, or have a discount on it. Don't pay twice. If in a couple (or a family) you can save money by getting personal cover – this covers the driver and all accompanying passengers whatever car is being driven.

Could you be an advanced driver?

If you take an advanced driving test, you can save money on insurance. It will cost you to take the test, but then most insurance companies will reduce your premium by around 20% if you take it and pass. The training and test costs upwards from £99 (depending on the way you train and take the test). **Advanced-driving.co.uk** has all the details.

The AA offers free driver training to newly qualified drivers who passed their test in the last twelve months. Completing this extra training can also save you on insurance.

Cheaper insurance for women drivers – despite the EU's ruling?

In 2011, the EU ruled that offering cheaper car insurance to women drivers because of their better overall safety record was discriminatory. So insurers are no longer able to offer anyone cheaper car insurance because of their sex. But they are still allowed to have companies called Sheila's Wheels, brand their websites entirely in pink, with pictures of diamonté-clad ladies driving luminous pink cars, and then sell cheaper insurance to the people who buy from their site, who, strangely enough, all happen to be women. So, guys, Sheila's Wheels don't have to just be for Sheilas.

Cheapest petrol and long journey supplies

Check out **petrolprices.com** or download the app for your phone to find out the cheapest prices for petrol for wherever you are. Before a long journey, fill up at your cheapest local garage so as not to buy petrol at motorway stations, as the fuel there is much more expensive (saving 5p per litre on a full tank which holds fifty litres can save you £2.50 each time you fill up).

If you must buy petrol from motorway service stations, don't buy anything else – *Which?* found that a WH Smith's bottle of water at a service station costs over 90% more than one bought in high street shops. Plan ahead before long journeys – filling up with petrol, water, snacks etc. from shops with sensible prices.

Petrol promotions

Supermarkets often have petrol promotions such as 'spend £50 in-store or online and get 5p off every litre'. Keep an eye out for these, do a big grocery shop and save about £2.50 on a full tank of petrol. Some petrol stations may have a loyalty scheme, which may save you money – but don't be loyal at any price, as you may find their petrol more expensive than at another station.

Eco-driving – it's easy when you know how

You can save 10–30% on fuel bills just by driving better, according to the AA's eco-driving study (**theaa.com**). This means that on an average mileage, per year you could save £100–£300 just by driving better:

👍 Accelerate and decelerate more slowly – just this eco-driving measure alone can save 5% off your fuel bill. Cars use a lot of fuel to accelerate quickly, and because of engine braking they also actually use fuel to decelerate. So try to keep your car rolling along, rather than stopping and starting

👍 Change gear earlier – most of us change gears later than we should and stand to save significant amounts of fuel by changing up earlier. The optimum rpm to change up a gear is 2,000 in a diesel car and 2,500 in a petrol car. Drive in the correct gear to save the car labouring and therefore using up more fuel, and brake slowly so the car uses its stored momentum

👍 Stick to the limits because speed costs – at high speeds your car uses much more than 10% more fuel to go 10% faster. According to the Department of Transport, driving at 80mph uses 25% more fuel than cruising at 70mph. When you burn rubber, you burn money too

👍 Be less idle – by idling less. The fuel cost of starting up an engine versus the fuel cost of keeping an engine going is overweighed after three minutes – i.e. if you're in a queue which looks like not moving for more than three minutes, then switch the engine off

👍 Remove extra drag items from the car when you don't need them (roof racks, bike racks etc.). Having windows open also causes drag on your car (but saves money versus the cost of using air con!)

👍 Turn the air conditioning down and the heated windows and other electricals off whenever possible. If it's really hot and you need air con, switch it on whilst bringing in air from outside, then turn it off and circulate the air round inside the car for a while. Using your air con increases your fuel costs by 10% – only use when essential

Coasting *isn't* saving

Coasting (turning off the engine) when driving downhill is not advisable. It's unsafe, and the methods of fuel injection in modern cars mean that it doesn't even save you fuel any more.

Look after your car

Keep your tyres inflated as lower pressure increases the drag on the car, meaning you use up more fuel. Check your car regularly for oil and water to make sure it's running as efficiently as possible. Don't ignore a warning light, as your engine could be suffering and the repair bill could follow fast on the warning light's heels. Keep your car clean and tidy to protect its value when you come to sell it on or part exchange.

Servicing your car

Shop around for a garage to service your car which will offer you a good deal. Look out for promotions from garages trying to drum up new customers. If you have a friend who is handy take them with you when taking your car to a garage to be serviced – this can cut down your chances of being hoodwinked by a garage on the make.

Parking

In major cities, parking can be a major headache and expense but:

👍 Electric cars are entirely exempt from parking charges in many cities, which is another great reason to get one

👍 Check out the websites **parkatmyhouse.com**, **yourparkingspace.co.uk** and **parkonmydrive.com** for short-term parking slots, or **parklet.co.uk** for longer term parking, which will cost you much less than expensive pay-and-display parking or car park prices

👍 You can save ££s by avoiding expensive airport car parks and instead renting a space from someone nearby

You can also use these websites to make money out of a parking space or garage that you might have, especially if it's in a frequently used spot.

Parking fines

Parking tickets are the bane of many car owners' lives – the two-minute stop which costs you £60 in a parking fine. Always challenge parking tickets if you think they are unfair – e.g. if a sign is unclear or obscured, or, as can happen, downright wrong compared to the ticket issued. Take photographs of any surrounding evidence, and copy your letter to your MP. Often the borough or county will back down with a written 'don't do it again' warning.

BIKE IT

On your bike

There are no congestion charges for cycling, no parking tickets or fines, no insurance or tax, and it keeps you fit too. There is a lot to be said for cycling, and **sustrans.org.uk** has said most of it. They are the charity behind the National Cycle Network and their website has heaps of info on cycle routes near you, tips for cycling with children, and guides to choosing the perfect bike for you. Also check out **cyclemaps.org.uk** for downloadable printable maps of cycle routes around the country.

Cheap bikes

New bikes cost around three times as much as the equivalent refurbished bike in good condition, check **yell.com** or **freeindex.co.uk** for refurbished cycle shops in your local area. A refurbished bike from a shop should have been fully serviced. Ex-hire bikes are often very good value and the hire outlet will service them so they look almost new – check cycle hire in **yell.com** to find your nearest service.

On someone else's bike

Be sure to check if your local area, or an area you are travelling to, has a bike borrow scheme, as many places do, e.g. London, Blackpool, Cardiff, Reading, Farnborough, Newcastle, Nottingham. New schemes are being created all the time. There are schemes all round the world including in Ireland, many dozen in Europe, but also several in the USA, China and Japan. Wikipedia has a full list of cities with schemes: **http://en.wikipedia.org/wiki/List_of_bicycle_sharing_systems**. Some car parks in France lend bikes to customers parking cars. Each scheme is different – check carefully the charge for each time period for your scheme.

If you want to use a bike for a particular period, such as a week, check out **ecomodo.com** *to borrow one for less than the cost of buying, or if you have a bike to loan out, here is where to find someone who might need it.*

On your electric bike

Pedal when you can, and let the battery take the strain when you can't. Much, much cheaper than petrol, but much less likely to give you sweaty work clothes than riding a pedal bike, an electric bike can save you money – if you use it to replace journeys you would have taken by car, and especially if it enables you to ditch the car altogether. These cost £900 upwards, but then with a rechargeable battery the running costs are very small. Check out **electricbikesales.co.uk/info/buyingguide and pedelecs.co.uk** for reviews and tips on going electric.

You will need to invest in seriously good locks if you buy a motorbike, scooter or bicycle as these are tempting to steal.

On your work's bike

Join your company's Cycle to Work scheme, if they have one, or suggest they start one if they don't. This nationwide scheme enables employers to loan bikes and accessories to employees as a tax-free benefit. This means that you could have use of a bike with accompanying lights, helmet, cycle clips, panniers etc., loaned to you from your company without you having to pay for any of it.

The bike and accessories would be the property of the company and you would be expected to use it to reach work, but you are fully entitled to use it for non-work journeys as well. Riding the bike to a station and then taking the train without it is counted as a journey to work. In fact, the company could provide you with two bikes if you argued you needed them – e.g. one to ride to a station, and one at the destination station to ride into work. Electric bikes are also included. There is no limit on the total value of the equipment and bike that can be loaned.

TRAVELLING BY TRAIN OR BUS

Book twelve weeks early

Rail companies usually release their cheapest seats twelve weeks before departure dates. Use **thetrainline.com**'s ticket alert system (at the bottom of its homepage) to be notified exactly when advance tickets will come on sale for a particular journey.

Even if it's not early, still book

If you can't book weeks or even days early, it's still worth booking a ticket online or over the phone the moment before you set off for the station – you will almost certainly get a better deal than buying at the station.

Megatrain

Megatrain, **uk.megabus.com/megatrain**, sells tickets for £1 for a selected number of long-distance journeys, e.g. London to Liverpool. The fares can really be as cheap as £1 when you book weeks in advance. And fortunately, Megatrain sells bucket-priced tickets but doesn't run bucket trains – you will be travelling on the same Virgin or East Coast (etc.) train as everyone else who paid full-price for their tickets.

Single or return?

👍 Return fares should be the cheapest, but sometimes two singles can be cheaper than a return, especially if you can buy even one as an advance cheap fare single. So always check.

👍 Conversely, a return ticket can be cheaper than a single, so could be worth getting even if you are only making a one-way journey.

Booking

Booking direct with the train companies or through the National Rail Enquiries website (**nationalrail.co.uk**) will incur you no booking fee, unlike **thetrainline.com** and other pooling companies which all charge booking fees. But although **thetrainline.com** and other pooling companies such as **raileasy.co.uk** do charge booking fees, they often sell much cheaper tickets, so worth checking out.

Promotions

👍 National Rail Enquiries website also has promotions covering all the train companies – click on train times and tickets and then special offers and see where you can go for an adventure on the cheap

👍 Virgin often have special promotional fares but they are often harder to find than on other websites so check carefully. Check out their website **virgintrains.co.uk**

👍 East Coast Trains always carry a range of promotions – e.g. $1/3$rd off advance tickets for groups of three or more, 25% off the purchase of a national railcard, 20% off parking at certain stations etc. Check the special offers button on their website (**eastcoast.co.uk**)

> *Travelling between London and Scotland? Save on a night's accommodation by taking the Caledonian Sleeper with Scot Rail – they have bargain berths from £19 if you book in advance.*

Cheaper bites on the go

Register for a bitecard at **bitecard.co.uk** and you can get a 20% discount off all purchases at many of the food and drink outlets at mainline railway stations and some coach stations.

Split ticketing

The train fares system in the UK is insanely complicated and often seemingly nonsensical, but it's about to sound even more so – if you haven't heard of it already, welcome to the world of split ticketing.

It can often be considerably cheaper to buy several tickets adding up to a whole journey, rather than the single big ticket. For example, to go from Oxford to Edinburgh, rather than buy a return ticket for that journey, you can make great savings by splitting the tickets at Wolverhampton, i.e. buying four singles – Oxford to Wolverhampton, Wolverhampton to Edinburgh, Edinburgh to Wolverhampton and then Wolverhampton to Oxford.

Split ticketing is totally legal and you don't have to get off the train at the split station, but you must make certain that the trains you will be travelling on are due to stop at the stations you split the tickets at. You have to do the legwork yourself on the National Rail Enquiries or train carriers' website – don't try to ask for help from a ticket office, neither of you will enjoy the conversation.

Tricks for split ticketing

👍 If part of your journey is during peak time but part not, try to split the ticket so that you can purchase a cheap advance ticket for the non peak time section

👍 Check if you can purchase a Megatrain ticket for any part of your journey

One trick you might think of but shouldn't try is buying a ticket for a journey that is longer than the journey you intend to make – e.g. Banbury to London is cheaper than Oxford to London, so why not buy Banbury to London but board at Oxford? Answer: because it's against the terms and conditions of the tickets and if they find you, they'll fine you.

Tricks for pleasanter train travel

👍 If you have a standard purchase ticket (i.e. not an advance ticket) you can upgrade to first class for £10 at the weekend with most train companies. Cross Country Trains lets you buy this option on their website

👍 Some long-distance routes still have dining carriages, and these are always located in first class. If your train does, and you are hungry enough for dinner, you can shimmy into first class, even if you're travelling with children, and eat good food at reasonable prices while sinking into your comfortable first-class seat. In theory, the staff could return you to standard class when you have finished your meal, but in practice they rarely do

 If you are on a very overcrowded train (not at commuter times but, for example, a bank holiday weekend) the guard will often let standard-class travellers sit in first class if there is space and you ask them very nicely

Complain

If your train is late you are entitled to a full or partial refund, depending on the length of journey and the quantity of lateness. Keep all the parts of your ticket (i.e. including the receipt part that the machines dispense) and pick up a reclaim form if your train is more than thirty minutes late.

Railcards and season tickets

Railcards – e.g. Senior Railcard, Friends and Family Railcard, etc. – will save you money if, on average, you make more than four rail journeys a year. Check out the latest cards on the National Rail Enquiries website: **railcard.co.uk**.

Also check there for the season ticket calculator to see if you make a journey frequently enough for a season ticket to save you money.

Check if your employer has a scheme to loan you the money for an annual season ticket – i.e. they pay the lump sum and you pay back one-twelfth of it each month. If they don't have such a scheme suggest they start one.

Europe

InterRail passes can save you money on European travel if you plan carefully how many days you will travel for.

Meanwhile **Seat61.com** is the authority for prices and times for travelling around Europe by train and boat.

Buses

As well as the ubiquitous National Express there are now several very cheap bus operators around the country – Greyhound UK, Terravision, Easybus, Megabus, and Megabusplus, which combines bus and train travel on some routes.

All OAPs (over-sixties) are now entitled to a bus pass, which gives free travel on all local bus routes across the country.

London tube and bus travel

In London, fares on the bus or tube with an Oyster card are around 30% cheaper than buying on board the bus or at ticket machines at bus stops or stations. So even if you visit for only a few days, it's worth buying an Oyster card (on sale in any tube station for a £3 deposit, plus whatever money you load it with).

SUMMARY

Save the expense of buying a car – rent one for the day from a car club, or from a private individual who is hiring theirs out. Avoid the big car parks and instead use the Internet to find someone who is renting out their drive for a fraction of the cost. Get on your bike for green, clean travel that keeps you fit too – or better still persuade your employer to buy you a bike. Make sure you register for free bus travel if you're over sixty, and for an Oyster card if you live in or visit London. If you're travelling by train, be sure to check the promotions that the different rail companies are offering, and if you have the courage to enter the complicated world of split ticketing, you can save ££s.

18. Luxuries: Going Out

SAVE MONEY BUT STILL HAVE FUN

Groupon etc.

In these days of vouchers and two-for-one deals, the best way to treat yourself or friends and family to an evening out or a day trip is to choose to go somewhere where you can get a great deal. Start by registering with **groupon.com** to be emailed or texted deals operating today for wherever you are. If you are travelling around the country, register again with the location you will be visiting. Also check out the latest vouchers and cheap ticket deals online, for example at **moneysavingexpert.com**.

Drinks for less

The prices charged by pubs, even chain pubs, vary hugely across the country. A pint of beer can cost 50% less in a small pub or working man's club in the north of England than in a busy bar in central London. Seek out the cheaper places near you.

Happy hour times vary but they mostly take up the early slot when customers are few – if you can, shift your evening out to start at five or six p.m. so you can take advantage. Check out the times of some good places near you. For London, **viewlondon.co.uk** has a list of happy hours for specific venues and times.

Eating out for less

Stacks of restaurants offer semi-permanent two-for-one deals, such as Strada, Pizza Express and Café Rouge, so always check out their websites if you're looking for a meal out.

Note that vouchers are not restricted to chain restaurants: many independent restaurants have joined in on the act in a bid to gain customers. Check out the deals on **quidco.com**, **groupon.com** and **moneysavingexpert.com** for printable vouchers to take along to the restaurant.

Late lunches can save you £££s, as many chain restaurants, e.g. Pizza Hut, offer discounts and special rates for eating between 3 and 6 p.m.

Living social

Register at **livingsocial.com** for their daily emails to your computer or phone of big discounts on restaurants, spas and so on close to you. To get a deal, you need to buy it in advance, so you have to commit to going to your chosen venue. But if you then share the deal and three other people buy it, it is free for you. This also means that the saving for eating out with a large group is huge.

Tipping

Instead of simply paying the automatic tip added to the bill by the restaurant owner, pay the bill without this tip and then leave a tip in cash. This way you can be sure the tip goes directly to your server, otherwise the restaurant owners often cream off up to half of these tips, splitting the rest between all staff. You can actually leave less of a tip this way and yet more money goes to your server, who might remember you for next time and give you that nice table in the corner.

Day-tripping out for less

From National Trust castles to theme parks there are masses of two-for-one and other ticket discount deals to be had. National Rail has oceans of deals including two tickets for the price of one for many attractions, e.g. Sea Life Centre Birmingham, Madame Tussauds, Alton Towers, London Zoo, London Dungeon – see their **daysoutguide.co.uk** site for all current offers. You have to book a train ticket to get the offer, but any train ticket will do, so if you wouldn't plan to travel by train, just buy a cheap £2 or £3 train ticket, which will still make the deal worthwhile.

If you can't find a special offer for where you want to go, still check out the venue's website in advance, as very often you will save money by booking online rather than just turning up and paying for entrance.

Check for your region

- Many regional tourist boards have two-for-one offers for local attractions, e.g. see **southeastoffers.com**, or **visittheheart.co.uk** for offers in the Midlands, or **visitwales.co.uk** for Welsh offers, etc.

- **EnjoyEngland.com** reviews the best travel apps for all regions of the country and modes of travel to help you get about

London attractions

Most of London's art galleries and museums are entirely free. If you do want to visit paying attractions in London, then check out **discount-London.com** for special offers on many of London's top tourist sites. If you are planning a serious amount of sightseeing, look at **Londonpass.com** and see if you can save money by buying a ticket which then gives you free entry to over fifty London attractions, without queuing when you reach the attraction. Prices are, for example, around £58 for an adult pass for two days, and sometimes other websites will offer a London Pass card at a discount, e.g. check **allinlondon.co.uk**.

Shows for free

Tickets for top shows can go for seriously top prices. But you don't need to pay top dollar to see great entertainment. You can get to see a great number of TV shows, theatre and dance shows for absolutely nothing.

Be the audience

The BBC issues tickets for free to watch a whole host of TV and radio programmes being recorded all over the country – apply at **bbc.co.uk/tickets**. Often programmes are over-subscribed, so bid for several shows to see what you can get.

You can get to be in the audience for audition shows like *The X Factor*, *Britain's Got Talent*, *Sing If You Can*, etc., as well as comedy panel shows – register at **applausestore.com**. Also try **lostintv.com**, **SROaudiences.com** and **tvrecordings.com** for other comedy and entertainment TV programmes.

Often these companies over-book audiences to make sure they are full, so arrive an hour early to be sure of your seat. Also, seating is first come first served, so be early to be near the front.

Be the press

Major live theatre, comedy and dance shows have preview nights before the real opening night. These are reserved for people in the press, with the idea that they will review the show. If you run a successful blog, or have many followers on Twitter, or are part of a school or work newsletter, you can phone theatre venues directly and ask if they have any spare tickets for preview nights.

Booking secrets for cheap tickets for shows

- The cheapest way to book tickets for theatre shows is usually in person at the venue (no booking fee) or online direct with the box office (either no fee or a low fee)

- The next cheapest option is by telephone direct with the box office

- Last of all use the ticket agencies, which often have rapacious booking fee charges, and might charge a higher price than the actual seat price

- Always book the cheap band of tickets if you can. If a show is selling poorly and doesn't have a big audience, they often close the cheap part of the theatre for that evening's performance, moving everyone down into the more expensive seats for no added cost

👍 Do check out the National Rail website **daysoutguide.co.uk** for two-for-one deals on theatre tickets – you have to buy a train ticket for the offer, but you can buy any ticket, e.g. even for £2–3

👍 **Lastminute.com** has many cheap deals for shows including £10 tickets. They also offer many restaurant-and-show combined deals, which can save you £££s on a great night out. To be notified of special offers and priority booking, register for email updates from your favourite venues

👍 Do check out performances at fringe/amateur venues as they often have great shows on for a fraction of West End prices, and sometimes you can catch a hit this way before it has become a hit and transfers to a high-priced venue

For shows in London, be sure to check the half-price ticket booth in the middle of Leicester Square (not the ticket agencies around the sides of the square). The half-price ticket booth sells half-price tickets for that day's performance for many London shows.

The royal box?

Always check the price of boxes in theatres – because they have a side view of the stage, these are often almost the cheapest seats in the house, but the advantage is you have an uninterrupted view and your own private velvety lined box too. Check **theatremonkey.com** for advice on the best value seats in many London theatres.

Students and young people

For students, most theatres have student prices, so do check. The Royal Opera House sells student tickets for only £10 for non-sold-out shows.

The Arts Council has organized free tickets for under twenty-sixes for hundreds of venues and shows across the country – check out **anightlessordinary.org.uk**. You can only be allocated one ticket per person, so if you want to go with friends, you need to contact the venue directly to arrange several tickets for the same show.

Tickets for gigs

Register as a fan on your favourite band's website and you should be immediately notified for tours and given the first options to buy tickets. There are a huge number of fake tickets sold for every gig, so be wary when you buy from anything other than the official website.

That said, **scarletmist.com**, a free peer-to-peer ticket exchange site, is designed to enable trade from one fan to another, cutting out the middleman or the tout. But always make all reasonable checks.

Look at **safefromscams.co.uk** *for help on identifying scams.*

Cinema

Cinema companies regularly offer two-for-one deals – check out the voucher offers in **moneysupermarket.com** or **freestuffjunction.co.uk** to find the latest deals. Also you can get two tickets for the price of one every Wednesday at cinemas nationwide through the phone company Orange. To get the deal, text FILM to number 241; the text costs 35p.

Cheap seats at Vue

Vue cinemas do tickets for children for only £1.25 at weekends and in school holidays, and family tickets where two adults pay the same price as the children. Vue also do teen rates – £2 for thirteen- to eighteen-year-olds every Thursday and Friday, and accompanying adults pay the same price. Also some Vue cinemas do a 'cheap day' offer in return for a small survey from you. Check if your local Vue participates.

See a preview for free

You can go and see a preview of a film for free if you register with screening companies. The reason they get you along is to know how well the film will go down at the box office, so they usually want to hear your feedback after. This means you get to see a film for free and play at being a critic for the day too.

Register with **showfilmfirst.com**, **seefilmfirst.com**, **momentumscreenings.co.uk**, **disneyscreenings.co.uk**. When films become available, you are emailed with a code which you enter on their website to get your free ticket.

Attendance allowance at cinemas

Those receiving the disability living allowance or who are registered blind are entitled to the attendance allowance on cinema trips to enable their carer to come with them for free. The person cared for needs to apply and the card costs £5.50 per year and enables two-for-one cinema tickets for over 500 cinemas across the country. The person in care must then buy one full-priced ticket showing the card at the cinema, enabling their carer to get in free.

Festivals for free

Register in the deep mid winter and you can have some festival fun in the summer in return for a little of your time and effort. Festivals don't run themselves and you could do some shifts providing security or litter collection or car park organizing or pulling pints ... and then spend the rest of the time watching the music and soaking up the atmosphere for free.

Oxfam recruits volunteers to work in their festival shops, to campaign at the festival and to be festival stewards at the country's biggest festivals such as Glastonbury, Womad, Bestival, etc. You have to do three shifts over the course of the festival and pay a deposit of £185 – you get this back at the end of the festival season as long as you turn up and carry out all your shifts. You only need to pay one deposit to volunteer for as many festivals as you like.

Other companies to try to get work with at festivals are: the Workers Beer Company, **workersbeer.co.uk** ('thirst among equals' is their catchphrase), who run the beer tents; DC Site Services, **dcsiteservices.com**, who offer security; **networkrecycling.co.uk** for festivals' recycling needs; and **hotboxevents.com** who are hot on tent-pitching and directions advice.

Sport

Sporting events need casual labour too, so for free access to your favourite sporting venue, check out the options for working there. **Wimbledon.com**, for example, shows the many options for working at the tennis championships, whether as a driver, a steward, or in catering. You don't get seats for matches but once you are in the venue for free, there are usually lots of opportunities to enjoy the sport without having a seat.

Sporting facilities for free

Launched in 2006 to encourage more kids and adults to play tennis, **tennisforfree.com** now has free tennis playing at over 2,000 courts nationwide, and a few free coaching programmes. For kids only, **asda-sportingchance.co.uk** offers free sports classes nationwide in school holidays, and **tesco.com/football** has the same offer of free coaching for football.

SUMMARY

There are many ways to go out and see great entertainment for far less than the ticket price – be the audience and see a recording of a TV or radio show for nothing, review a show and watch it for free, or work a few shifts at a festival or a sporting event and have your entrance paid for. Sign up to be updated on the latest gigs by your favourite band or orchestra and you might be eligible for discounts on booking. And register for vouchers for all sorts of great deals for a variety of places to eat and drink.

19. Luxuries: Health and Beauty

BEAUTIFY WITHOUT THE EXPENSE

Face creams

Ditch the expensive creams and the whole panoply of moisturizers, age-defyers, and other associated paraphernalia which the pharmaceutical industry tries to goad us into buying, and instead buy the actual root product of most of these creams – i.e. standard dermatological creams which cost £3–4 for a massive 500g tub and are available from every local chemist. These don't have glamorous sounding names like Power Surge Moisturizing Balm or Rich Nourishing Skin Enhancer, but rather uninviting names like Aqueous Cream, Diprobase cream, and my personal favourite name, Unguentum Merck (although this is more pricey at £15, albeit for a huge 500g jar).

You will find that the root of most skincare creams is created from one standard medical cream or another – check the ingredients of your favourite expensive cream and compare with those in the big, cheap tubs in the chemist. These items are prescribed to moisturize skin conditions, which proves that they work. But you can just buy them over the counter and they are good for everybody's skin.

Try the smallest pots of these that your chemist will sell and see which suits your skin best. Then buy a huge tub for a small price, add a little sweet-smelling oil if you wish, and decant into an old, cleaned out, nice tub of posh branded cream which is lying around your house.

Skin solutions

Add deep moisture to your skin without going deep into your pocket:

👍 Olive oil is great for the skin; add a drop of lavender oil so that you're not confused with salad

👍 Easier to put on than olive oil, and odourless, is another hard-core medical cream which all good chemists sell, called 50:50 (50% liquid paraffin, 50% white soft paraffin). This provides lots of moisture for the skin

👍 Good quality honey can be smoothed onto your face and left there for fifteen minutes as a natural face mask which soaks deep into the skin and boosts natural moisture

Make-up cleansers for less

There is no need to buy make-up cleansers; a gentle non-soap cleaner such as Aqueous cream will do the job just as well. Another way to become clean and smell nice without troubling the beauty aisles is to buy a big bag of plain oatmeal from a supermarket's basic range. Blitz it in the blender to prevent it blocking the drain, then take this lovely load of dirt-cheap Scottish goodness into the shower or bath with you and literally rub all over. You exfoliate, clean, and get scented all at the same time. Remarkable but true.

Make your own

For other ideas on making your own beauty products, have a look at **makeyourcosmetics.com** for cosmetic 'recipes', and use **gracefruit.com** to buy the raw materials of a lot of make-up, such as mica powder. You can also make your own soap with lovely smellies and without any nasties – check out **candleandsoap.about.com** or **teachsoap.com**.

Fill up on freebies

Make the most of the brilliant sample giveaways in department-store beauty halls. Show a cursory interest in what they have to offer and ask for a sample to try before you commit to spending anything. Try it out on a few counters and your make-up bag will be full of freebies in no time.

Beauty from within, the easy way

For better, shinier skin, look to what you eat as much as what you put on the surface of the skin – consuming olive oil, fish oils, protein, fresh fruit and vegetables and lots of water will give your skin a boing and a bounce that the adverts for expensive treatments would be proud of. Feed your skin from the inside – because you are indeed worth it.

Be (well) treated by a trainee

Rather than go to a quick cheapy barber, help the next generation. Most hairdressers will have students cutting hair at a fraction of the cost of a regular stylist. They will usually do you just as good a cut, but they will take several times as long because they are supervised by the professionals, so allow several hours, bring a good book and save ££s. Beauty schools are another good port of call – they often have commercial salons linked to them where you can receive treatments from trainees for much less than the regular rate, e.g. in London look up the **lcbt.co.uk** where a 75-minute massage costs just £20.

Vouchers

Treatments, such as massages, facials, haircuts etc., are very frequently featured on a lot of the voucher sites (**groupon.com**, **livingsocial.co.uk** etc., as on pages 19 and 20). Register with these and treat yourself for less.

Loyalty cards

Most salons use loyalty cards offering a treatment for free after a certain number of paid treatments. Be sure always to have your treatment put on your card so you are eligible, and when cashing in your card, be sure you are claiming the best value you can (e.g. with some salons you are best off having different loyalty cards for different priced treatments, but some will add up the prices of your treatments and offer you the average price for free).

Home medicaments

👍 Frozen peas make a great ice pack for injuries

👍 Bicarb is effective for neutralizing bee stings, while vinegar is good for treating wasp stings (*not* the other way around as bicarb is bad news for wasp stings)

👍 Moisturizer is just as good for sunburnt skin as dedicated products

White vinegar is also good for sunburn – spray it on a tissue and drape over the skin – the mild acidity helps restore acids in the skin and has a cooling effect

SUMMARY

From vouchers, loyalty cards and beauty schools, to cutting the massive pharmaceutical industry out of the equation by making your own make-up and moisturizers or soaps and smellies – there are plenty of ways to treat your beautiful self to beauty treats for less.

20. Family

'ALL YOU NEED IS LOVE.' **THE BEATLES**

SAVING FOR THE FUTURE GENERATION

Babies

Babies cost a fortune. Everyone knows that. How can things so tiny be so very expensive? The answer is partly because of the impulse to buy every bit of kit going, and partly because of babies' constantly changing needs and size. So, first job is to cut down on mother and baby purchases to what you actually need, and second job is to find ways for baby to grow without stretching the bank account.

Making maternity wear go further

Further round the growing bump, that is. Maternity wear needn't cost a lot – a mum-to-be needs expandable trousers and a floaty top. With these items, you can team regular favourite blouses or jumpers and then accessorize like mad with scarves and beads to beguile the eye away from the same old trousers or tunic.

👍 You can adapt your regular trousers to wear during pregnancy. Start by unbuttoning the trousers and sewing another button across the gap from the original button, then hook a rubber band over the new button. Result – extra inches of growth with no expense. Wear with longish tops so no one notices. When the bump grows so much that the zip needs to be undone, you can buy a 'bump band' from any maternity shop to cover the top of the trousers and it will just look like an extra layer

👍 You can buy 'bra extenders' for a few pounds from a haberdasher or department shop to prolong the life of bras through pregnancy rather than having to buy new ones

👍 Wrap-around skirts or dresses can be worn up until late into pregnancy, and then again after the baby is born. If you can't find any to buy, they are very easy to make – for advice on this, and ideas on adapting clothes for pregnancy wear, see **makeforbaby.com**

Buying maternity clothes

If you want to buy some pregnancy clothes, choose cheaper shops because you will wear them for such a short time:

👍 H&M do a good cheap range

👍 The National Childbirth Trust (NCT) has a 'nearly new sale finder' where maternity clothes or baby clothes can be sourced, visit **nct.org.uk/branches/event-finder**

👍 Fara is a superb charity shop specializing in mother and baby clothes – check out their locations at **faracharityshops.org**

All the baby equipment you don't need – and the few bits you do

The baby essentials are clothes, nappies, a buggy and a cot. All the rest you can do without or slim down on to cut costs.

Things you DON'T need to buy

A MOSES BASKET

Many buggies have an option to clip on a carrycot. As long as these meet safety requirements for sleep, they can function as the baby's first bed – all three of mine slept for their first several months in the carry cot.

AN EXPENSIVE COT

For baby's comfort and safety you need a new mattress in a cot, but the cot itself can be a second-hand or an old wooden cot, e.g. bought from eBay for very little. Clean it and paint it for a whole new lease of life.

SPECIAL LINEN

Not only does baby not need matching linen, they also don't need special fitted linen for the cot or pram – it's much cheaper to buy a new single or double bed sheet and cut and hem to make several cot or junior bed sheets than to buy dedicated ones.

A DECORATED NURSERY

Parents are seduced by adverts into believing that baby's room should be painted in pastel shades with children's characters marching round the walls. Baby will have to be over a year before they even notice the walls, and a lot older before they express a preference.

A COT BED

If you're planning on more than one child, don't buy a cot that turns into a cot bed as regular cots are much cheaper and by the time your child is ready for a cot bed, you might have another who is ready for their cot. You can then get a junior bed, which is cheaper than a converted cot bed. The moral of the story is, dual-function things are more expensive, so unless you can get great use from *both* functions, it can be better to get two different things to do each function.

AN EXPENSIVE HIGHCHAIR
Rather than buying a big plastic or wooden highchair that takes up space in the kitchen and/or at the table, buy a bucket seat highchair that clips onto a table. It also doubles up as a travel highchair. These sell for around £18, e.g. from **overstock.com**.

A CHANGING TABLE OR BAG
These take up space, are expensive and babies need constant supervising when on them. Change the baby on a mat on the bed instead – comfier, free and safer. There is no need for a large changing mat either – there are great foldable changers, e.g. the Sunshine Kids Change and Go from **kiddisave.co.uk** for around £6 which you can use at home and out and about. Just put this in your regular bag (there is no need for an expensive changing bag either).

SWADDLING CLOTHS
Shops sell dedicated swaddling cloths to help new babies sleep better. Instead, just use a regular muslin or small cotton sheet and learn how to fold them the old-fashioned way to keep baby cosy – see the technique on **adviceforbaby.com/swaddling**.

CONSTANT SUPPLIES OF NEW CLOTHES
One huge cost for growing babies is clothes, as babies seem to grow out of their babygrows in no time at all. Instead of dressing baby in all the latest fashions:

👍 Go to charity shops where you can get nearly new but good quality clothes

👍 Gratefully accept hand-me-downs from friends' kids

👍 Get clothes on your local freecycle site

If the clothes are not quite your style you can sew on a button or two or add a trim to personalize them. Once you've moved away from the idea that your new child *has* to have new things, and once you've washed and ironed the newly received things, you won't look back.

Regular charity shops often have very few kids' clothes, making for an unrewarding hunt, so find charity shops which specialize in children's clothes, e.g. Fara, which has a number of specialized kids' clothing shops all over south England – see **faracharityshops.org**. You can also make clothes for babies or toddlers, for example see **makebabystuff.com** for patterns and advice.

A BABY MOULI

As with so many baby-marketed things, the regular version works just as well for half the price. No need to buy a baby mouli for baby's first months of food – use a regular blender on the maximum setting.

Things you DO need

For equipment that you do need, e.g. stairgates, try freecycle, freegle and so on – these are heavily weighted with children's products because children grow out of them so quickly. Failing this, try the discounted websites **kiddicare.com** and **kiddisave.co.uk**.

FRIENDS

Attend your local NCT antenatal classes. You will make contact with other people due a new baby at the same time as you, which can be very valuable for pooling ideas, sharing experiences, and finding support. Also make contact with your local school – this is a great way for finding trusted babysitters from experienced parents who have done the searching for you.

SLEEP

Get baby into a routine of a long sleep after lunch in their cot and you've got yourself two hours of free time with no childcare cost – I've written three books this way (including this one) over the course of having three babies!

> *For gadgets that can ease the life of a parent (such as a stars and sun alarm clock, which cleverly indicates to children after what time they are allowed to get up and wake their parents), check out* **gro-store.co.uk, overstock.com** *and* **phpbaby.com.**

CHILDREN

Toys

Constant demands for new toys are a major source of emotional and financial strain for parents. Here are some ways to make things easier:

FIND YOUR LOCAL LIBRARY – these often have children's toys and free music sessions, not to mention books aplenty. There are no fines nationwide on children's books from libraries returned late and children can also borrow DVDs and computer games for free.

FIND A TOY LIBRARY – there are over 1,000 toy libraries in the UK providing brilliant opportunities for us all to pool resources. Check out the National Association of Toy and Leisure Libraries to find one near you – **natll.org.uk**. Try to get your children to review their toy collection and work out what they could donate to a local school or hospital in return for a new toy – employ the one in, one out principle. Not only does this keep toy clutter down, it also helps children think about how much they have and/or need. Donate toy rubbish, i.e. dolls with missing limbs etc., to local scrap stores, which use unwanted broken items for arts and crafts – see **ReduceReuseRecycle.co.uk** for locations of scrap stores. These also often run good free workshops – fun, and they help children see how to reuse what we have.

BOOK SWAPS – many schools have book swap schemes which work very well. Not only do children get access to different books, the children can review the books, which helps them to engage even more with the content. If your school doesn't have one, suggest they start one.

LEARN ABOUT MONEY – teach your kids about money and they might not be so eager to spend yours:

- 👍 Make pocket money something that is earned – not a right

- 👍 Get them to give away old toys before Christmas and birthdays, and get them to sell big items like bikes to get new ones

- 👍 Get them saving, e.g. Halifax has a good children's savings account; or you might encourage them to save in order to buy a particular item they want

- 👍 Get them linked to children in developing countries to give them more awareness of how much they already have, e.g. with a charity like Plan International, **plan-uk.org**, your children can write letters or emails to a sponsored child in a country they choose in the developing world

Travelling with kids – are we there yet?

No, but we're getting there:

👍 Portable DVD players are very cheap these days and can be a godsend

👍 A free source of entertainment is to hide children's favourite toys in the weeks before a long journey, then unpack them from your travel bag once you've set off. They'll be so pleased to see them there's a chance they might forgive you for hiding them

👍 Always carry plenty of snacks and water so you don't get caught out with expensive airport/zoo shops. Supermarkets and 99p shops sell good metal water bottles – plastic ones are not meant to be re-used many times and they can be carcinogenic after many uses. Bring fruit that's less easily bruised – e.g. oranges, raisins, apples. Unless you're travelling on an aeroplane, carry a pocket penknife with you so that you can easily cut and share fruit

Kids' parties

The sky can be the limit for what people spend on their children's birthday parties and research by the sweet-maker Haribo has found that the average spend is almost £130. But there is no need to spend anything like that to give your kids and their friends a great birthday experience.

KEEP THE NUMBERS DOWN
Don't invite the whole class even if other parents do. With only ten or twelve kids, you can probably fit everyone into your home, and if you invite only six or eight you can take the children on a trip. Either way, you save hundreds of pounds on hiring a hall, decorating it, and booking an entertainer to fill it.

CRAFTS AND GAMES AT HOME

Organize crafts at home – collect different sized boxes from packaging in the weeks before and enough rolls of sellotape and pairs of scissors to go round, then sit down with the children and make robots. Or decorate wooden spoons with faces, making clothes for them out of scraps. A small craft kit with coloured feathers and googly eyes is all you need for the finishing touches.

Rope in other parents to help – they usually won't mind and it can be a fun and social experience for everyone. Party games can be just as well run by you, or another dad or mum, as by an entertainer, see **partydelights.co.uk** for countless ideas on party games.

TAKE THEM ON A TRIP

Most of the country's museums and art galleries are free and many of them do children's activities at the weekends too. The National Gallery in London and the National Galleries of Scotland run free art workshops for kids and parents every Sunday with excellent materials provided, not to mention front row access to superb art.

Many museums provide kids' activity trails which you pick up at the front desk and the kids run around with. If your local museums don't, visit in advance and create your own 'Spotting List' of items that the children need to tick off as they go round. A completed sheet wins them their party bag. Some places even provide a guide for a very low cost if you book a group, e.g. Tower Bridge in London charges only £10 extra for a guide for a group. Tickets in a group of six or more are £3 each and children under-five go free.

Take sandwiches for the kids – most museums and art galleries have a place where groups can eat their own food if you ask in advance, saving you money on expensive cafeterias.

HOMEMADE SAVES THE DAY

👍 Don't buy invites – handwritten ones by your child can be charming, or for quicker alternatives there are many websites that let you create free invitations to email, showing videos, photos, music and writing, such as **smilebox.co.uk**

👍 Party bags can be cheaply filled with multi-packs from pound shops or similar. For the bags themselves, try your local greengrocer for some paper bags. If you ask the cost to buy twenty or thirty, they will usually give them to you for free

👍 Or don't even give in to the party bag demon – put a slice of cake in a napkin and get a job lot of books and give them a book each to take home. The parents will thank you for cutting out the plastic and sweets

Buy children's books in bulk from **thebookpeople.co.uk** *and you save £££s – you can keep some books from a set for your children, and give away others as presents.*

CAKE TOP TIPS

A special birthday cake from a good bakery will cost upwards of £20 depending on size. You can buy a theme cake from a supermarket cheaper than this, but for just £2 or £3 you can buy a plain supermarket cake and let your child help you decorate it at home for a personalized look at a fraction of the cost.

For decorations, swiss rolls are very cheap – supermarkets' basic ranges sell them for less than 20p – and they are perfect for chopping up and making shapes on a stand-out cake design such as a train, a gingerbread house or a pirate's chest. Add chocolate buttons and smarties for details.

Supermarket fairy cakes are also very cheap, but look good when home-decorated and put on a cake stand (supermarkets sell pretty cardboard cake stands). Check out **easy-birthday-cakes.com** for hundreds of ideas.

IF ONLY A BIG PARTY WILL DO

If the birthday is in summer, make the party virtually free with a BYO picnic in a local park and your child can happily invite every friend they have ever made. Bring some sporting equipment along, e.g. cricket bat and stumps, and with the help of some other parents you can have an impromptu sports day.

For a winter birthday, check out your local cinema for a group kids' deal (e.g. Vue cinemas are £2 on Saturdays for kids). Swimming pools and sports centres often do birthday party deals which work out very good value for large numbers.

Presents from kids

Use the school photos that you have to buy as presents for family members. Get your child to stick the photo onto a piece of card and decorate around it to make a personal photo frame the relatives will appreciate more than the expensive school-provided one.

TEENAGERS

Managing money together

Encourage teenagers to earn and manage their own money to try to reduce how often they come to you demanding money with menaces:

- 👍 Help them with budgeting and work together to make a clear plan when they start earning from a part-time job. You can make suggestions about how their weekly earnings are split, e.g. perhaps suggest that 50% goes into a savings account (e.g. a college fund), 40% they spend on what they like, and perhaps 10% to charity. You could also suggest that you 'match' their savings and so show that you are saving for their future together

- 👍 Set out ground rules about what clothes or other expenses you pay for and what you expect them to pay for. Encourage them to keep a rough track of their income and expenditure in a small notebook

- 👍 Pay-as-you-go phones will give them a mechanism for tracking their expenses

Think long and hard before you give your teenagers credit cards or take out a contract phone deal for them.

Earning money

Under the age of thirteen, children can be employed in modelling, sports promotion, entertainment or do odd jobs for relatives or friends.

From the age of thirteen to sixteen in the UK, young people can do 'light work' such as babysitting, some shop work or paper rounds. (Local by-laws may set out what can or can't be done in a particular authority.)

From the age of sixteen, young people can do a variety of jobs, but not work in transport, a factory, a mine or a ship. Young people are entitled to the minimum wage from the age of sixteen.

If teens can't get a paid job outside the home, they can do deals with the adults in the house and earn some pocket money by extra duties cleaning, car washing, grass cutting, or selling some unwanted items in the house on eBay.

Students' books

There is no need for academic texts to be new. For a great resource for finding used texts for a fraction of the price of new, check out **thebookpond.com** which puts new students needing textbooks in touch with students from previous years who no longer have a need for theirs. The site charges no commission, and any postage is agreed directly between buyers and sellers.

SUMMARY

There are hundreds of things sold to new parents that their babies can very happily do without, and many children have hundreds of toys which they don't play with, all the while asking for more. Squeeze the retailers' profit while your wallet is untouched by sourcing baby equipment from freecycle, toys from toy libraries, maternity clothes adapted from regular clothes, and kids' parties held as a sports day picnic in the park. Work with teenagers to help them manage their money, and preferably persuade them into a part-time job so they can be earning some for themselves too.

21. Weddings

SAVE MONEY ON THE BIG DAY

The average wedding cost

Weddings can be staggeringly expensive. The average wedding in the UK costs a whopping £18,500. Slim down the big fat wedding and you can save £££££s. These are the biggest ticket items with their average spends:

Reception (venue, food and drinks)	£4,000
Honeymoon and first night hotel	£3,400
Evening reception	£2,500
(venue, food and drinks, entertainment)	
The bride's outfit	£1,590
Photography	£900
Video	£900
The groom's and others' outfits	£775

Around £500 each: flowers, balloons and decorations, transport, stationery, the wedding cake, wedding rings.

Shhh, don't tell them it's a wedding

For almost everything you buy for the wedding from the entertainment to the food, and even including the wedding cake, don't tell companies that it's for a wedding. They routinely double prices compared to any other special event, e.g. anniversary or birthday. You probably should let the photographer know though.

Wedding exhibitions

Don't go to a wedding exhibition – yes, the prices may undercut regular wedding shop prices, but because of that you are tempted to buy everything there, whereas a much cheaper plan is to avoid wedding shops altogether. Look at **diybride.com** and **ethicalweddings.com** for a whole range of ideas for saving on weddings.

Save ££££s on drinks

Hold the reception in a non-traditional wedding location and you can save ££££s on wine and food by bringing in your own rather than being tied to the venue's providers. Venues regularly charge 'corkage' fees of up to £60 per bottle of champagne if you bring your own drinks to encourage you to buy their overpriced inferior labels. Instead, find a venue that doesn't charge corkage and you can bring your own vanload of cheaper drinks from the Continent. Sourcing these can even make some use of the inevitable stag weekend.

The local council for where you want to be married will have a list of all approved wedding venues, usually posted on their website. This way you can find the cheap and cheerful venues rather than just the swanky ones that pay to list themselves on wedding venue websites.

Decorations

👍 If you have a church wedding, then try to make it around Easter time or some other festival so that the church will already be beautifully decorated

👍 Formal flower displays can look so – er – formal. Instead, pick out bunches of flowers that you like from your local florist to dress the church or registry office – big bunches of lilies in the summer or daffodils at Easter always look lovely and bright. Choose in-season flowers for the cheapest prices

👍 You don't need a florist's vases – scour charity shops for unusual containers and you can have an eclectic individual look while saving pounds

👍 Buttonhole flowers can be easily made yourself with a rose or carnation, three ivy leaves, some wire, green tape and a pin – check out **flower-arrangement-advisor.com** for 'how to' videos

👍 If you can, take the church flowers to the venue when you leave for the reception to avoid paying for decorative flowers twice

Check out **cheap-wedding-success.co.uk** *for lots of ideas on how to cut costs.*

Get friends to pitch in

👍 Ask around and you may find that someone's cousin or friend of a friend was a caterer in a former life, or is happy to take your wedding video

👍 Ask musical friends to play for you as their gift to you, or ask about performers at a music college, as students will be cheaper than bands you pick from the *Yellow Pages*

👍 Presents for bridesmaids or pages can be homemade gifts, or you can give them a souvenir photo in a frame after the wedding, which will mean a lot to them when they're older

The wedding car can be one you've borrowed from a friend, or just walk to the venue and give the people nearby a treat

Invitations

Wedding invitations that are created using a photograph of the happy couple are more likely to be enjoyed and kept by your guests rather than the traditional formal invitations. You can create a design yourself if you, or anyone you know, is good at Photoshop or other design software. Otherwise, a photo shop such as Snappy Snaps will come up with ideas and do the work for you for around £20 and then print them for £££s less than a traditional wedding stationer. Or create invitations for free – send them out by email and then people can print off their own.

The all-important photos

Is the photography so important that it has to be left to the professionals who charge £1,000 or more for the day? Yes, it is important, but there are alternatives:

 Speak to your local art college or university and ask for any photography students who may be interested – this way you can get the skill at a fraction of the price

 Newspapers are often a good source of talented photographers who might welcome some weekend work at a wedding – call your local newspaper and ask to speak to a photographer

 Negotiate with a photographer on exactly what they're charging you for. For example, a lot of the cost can be tied into expensive production of a glossy wedding album – ask if they'll quote you a discounted fee for

simply providing a disk of hi-res images instead. You can then make your own album yourselves if you wish, e.g. with a company like **myphotobook.co.uk**

👍 You may have a friend who is a dab hand with a camera, but if you do ask a friend to be the official photographer, it is a good idea to have asked a second friend to be on the case for photos too, preferably from the other side of the family, otherwise you can end up with hundreds of photos of the bride or groom's family, and none of the other. Again, if you ask a friend to do this, suggest this be their wedding present to you. They may even make the photos up into an album for you afterwards

Wonderful honeymoons that don't break the bank

Your honeymoon is set to be a magical romantic occasion – but does it have to be the most expensive holiday you ever take? Above all, the point is to have a wonderful time together – why not ask around if any friend or friend of a friend has a lovely house somewhere that you could stay in? Ask them to make this their wedding present to you.

Here comes the bride

The bride doesn't need the full meringue that takes eighteen months to order and ten fittings to look just right. It can just be a beautiful dress that the bride might be able to wear again. High street stores do lovely gowns for under £100.

For an individual wedding dress but without wedding shop prices, you can save ££££s by finding a dressmaker to make a wedding dress according to your, or someone else's, design. Graphically create a dress on **weddingdresscreator.com**. Don't look for wedding dress tailors or your price is doubled – any good dressmaker can make a dress that will look good on you if the design is right. Check out **yell.com** for local tailors or dressmakers in poorer parts of town and go and talk to them about your design.

Ebay is also worth a look for interesting and unusual wedding dresses at reasonable prices. The Internet also hosts 'once worn' sites for wedding dresses, e.g. **almostnewweddingdresses.co.uk**, so you could buy your dream designer dress for a fraction of its retail price. These sites are also worth exploring post-wedding if you choose to sell your dress.

Headgear

A fabulous fascinator to rival the £600 creations found in expensive bridal wear shops can be made from an alice band covered in a few pounds' worth of feathers, lace and netting from a good haberdasher. If you don't feel up to the task ask around – chances are you have a creative friend who will.

Remember the old adage about 'something borrowed' – many brides are happy to see their wedding accoutrements used again, so ask married friends if they could lend you veils, garters, shrugs, clutch bags, jewellery and so on.

Wedding shoes can be dyed black after the big day so that they can be worn again.

Grooms and bridesmaids

Again, avoid targeted wedding shops: the groom can wear a new suit, shirt and tie – or even just a new shirt and tie in brighter colours than he would usually wear to give a totally new look, even when paired with a suit he already owns.

With enough planning time before the wedding, you should be able to get bridesmaids' clothes in the sale for the right season – i.e. in the summer sales the year before the wedding, you can buy outfits for a summer wedding; in the January sales you can buy outfits for a spring or autumn wedding.

Wedding cake

Think outside the cake box and you will save £££s. Many bakeries do special cakes that look amazing, whereas their wedding cakes also look amazing but are two or three times as much. Check out the occasion cakes from Patisserie Valerie, **patisserie-valerie.co.uk**, which has branches across the country.

Alternatively, cupcake towers can look great. To cut the expense of bought cupcakes, you can buy them ready-made but undecorated from a supermarket and you or friends can decorate them and arrange them on a swanky cake display stand.

A gift of saving

The wedding day is one day at the start of a new life. Curb your wedding expenditure and prioritize your spending for the future, especially if it's important to save for a flat or a house.

There's nothing wrong with asking for wedding gifts to be money to go towards your life together. One couple I know say that what put them on a sound financial footing and enabled them to think about starting a family was the nest egg they built up from their wedding gifts.

SUMMARY

You can organize a super wedding without a super budget with ploys like doing your own flower arrangements, having friends pitch in to provide music or catering, finding a photographer from an art college or newspaper, and having a dress made by a local tailor – or buying one second-hand – for a good deal less than the boutique wedding shops. Avoid the targeted wedding shops altogether and you can have a great wedding for much less than the usual great expense.

22. Funerals

DEATH AND BEYOND

Making a will

No one likes to consider the demise of a loved one or of themselves, but death comes to us all and, as with everything else, things go more smoothly if they are planned. More than 60% of people in the UK haven't made a will, but whatever your age, if you have any assets such as a house or any savings or a business and you have any dependants, such as children, or any other people you would like to be looked after, then you should make a will. But there are plenty of alternatives to paying a lawyer for this.

A will for free, or for a donation to charity

It's easy to draw up your own will:

👍 You can buy a pack to do so from the Post Office or from a stationer's such as WH Smith

👍 You can have a lawyer draw it up for you for free if you are over fifty-five – there's a small scheme which organizes free wills each March and October. It runs for different towns each year, check out if you are close to a centre at **freewillsmonth.org.uk**

👍 Anyone over fifty-five can also have a will drawn up for free from Cancer Research UK, as can anyone over sixty from the Stroke Association

Or anyone can have a lawyer draw up a will at a cheap fixed rate and the money you pay goes to charity: each November is Will Aid month, check out **willaid.org.uk** for listings of solicitors who participate in Will Aid. You pay £75 for a single will, or £110 for a joint will, but all this money goes to charity – see how it is spent on the Will Aid website. There is a similar charity donation scheme which charges even less but operates for only Scottish residents – **willreliefscotland.co.uk**

Funerals

The basic cost of cremation is around £400 and burial in a coffin costs around £600. Extra costs such as a funeral director, hired car, headstone, flowers, choir, dress/suit hire, minister's fees, newspaper announcement, order of service and the coffin itself bring the average cost of a funeral to around £5,000. You can make substantial savings on this because a cheaper funeral is not necessarily a worse funeral.

Alternative options

Take a look at the **goodfuneralguide.com** and **mylastsong.com** for ideas on how to organize a funeral without the expense. There are alternatives to the traditional cemetery burial – such as a woodland burial. There are 200 woodland burial sites in the UK where a tree grows over the grave, rather than a headstone. They are also peaceful places to visit to remember loved ones, see **woodlandburialground.co.uk**.

Also the Natural Death Centre, **naturaldeath.org.uk**, has a list of natural burial grounds and ideas for saving money on a funeral. A person can also be buried on their own land or that of a friend: as long as no money changes hands, you don't need planning permission.

DIY RIP

There is no law against planning a funeral yourself and then you won't have funeral director costs. It does take a lot of planning, but may provide more 'closure' for you if you, or a group of you, take this on. Have a look at **funeralhelper.org** for advice on how to 'DIY a funeral'.

You can print out an order of service yourself with poems and hymns, and pick seasonal flowers from the garden or get some from the market, as wreaths and bouquets can be very expensive (£100 upwards). If the deceased is not very heavy, there's no reason why four ordinary people can't carry the coffin instead of pallbearers and you don't have to put it on shoulders so four women can easily manage a coffin.

Helping Hands

Usually after a death people ask, 'Is there anything I can do to help?' And you can say, 'Yes, please.' Friends can make sandwiches and cakes, provide the cutlery and crockery, organize the drinks and the tea and coffee. Catering for fifty people can quickly cost much more than £500, so delegate the job if you can.

To relieve relatives of any financial headache after a death, pre-paid funeral plans can be a good idea. Both the Co-operative and Nationwide offer good plans.

SUMMARY

You can be economical when planning funeral arrangements while still being sensitive to people's emotions. You can draw up a will yourself with a simple pack from a stationer's or the Post Office, or some charities provide them for free to pensioners, or there are schemes whereby you donate to a charity and a solicitor draws up a will for you. Funeral arrangements don't need to be undertaken by an undertaker, and burials on private land with permission are entirely legal. For catering at a wake, have friends pitch in to help.

23. Christmas

'TIS THE SEASON TO BE FRUGAL'

HOW TO SAVE MONEY AT CHRISTMAS

Budget

The average family spends over £600 celebrating Christmas.
So plan ahead – if you can spread the cost over several
months, it won't hit you so hard. If you do need to borrow
money, try to do it with a 0% card and pay back as much as
you can afford each month to avoid having to pay interest. If
you have a time-limited 0% card, make sure your debt is fully
paid off within the promotion period.

The government's website **consumerdirect.gov.uk** *has
a 'Save Xmas' campaign each year comparing the
different ways of saving for Christmas, including special
building society 'saving for Christmas' accounts.*

Cards

To send or not to send? That is the question:

👍 First of all, do the maths: fifty cards @ 50p each = £25, plus fifty second-class stamps @ 36p each = £18. So your outlay on fifty posted cards could be £43

👍 If you are posting cards, don't miss the last second-class posting date and find yourself paying 46p for a stamp (fifty of these comes to an annoying £23, making a total of nearly £50). And many people send many more than fifty cards

👍 If you do decide to send cards, you could cut up last year's cards and send them as postcards, so you only pay for the stamp

👍 Or if you choose to buy cards, **christmas-cards.org.uk** enables you to choose which charity 100% of the profits from the cards will go to

👍 Encourage children to make Christmas cards for their friends and family – **activityvillage.co.uk** has hundreds of ideas

👍 Consider e-cards, particularly for people who are borderline on the Christmas card list. Personalized e-cards with photos attached make a nice surprise in someone's inbox. Visit **smilebox.com** or the British Library, **bl.uk/ecards/**

Talk about it

Come to agreements with friends about whether or not you're going to give them presents/send cards. You might agree to give each other something each of you really wants or you might decide not to send cards at all but to give money to charity instead. Talk with friends or family and suggest that you buy them X but not until the January sales and you will save pounds.

Shopping for presents

Christmas is really very likely to come every year, so plan for it:

👍 Buy presents earlier in the year when you see goodies on special offer and squirrel them away for December

👍 Look out for vouchers and store discounts and stock up with food and presents in a Christmas cupboard or drawer

👍 Make things through the year for loved ones, or grab bargains at craft fairs and keep them by

👍 When you're shopping for presents, make a list and stick to it

👍 Shop around online to find the cheapest item (e.g. using shop bots, see Shopping: Make Technology Work for You, page 16) and order well enough in advance so that you can buy it with cheaper, rather than speedier and more expensive, delivery

👍 Stock up through the year with cheap ribbon, card and envelopes

Don't be caught out just the week before the 25th with nothing in the cupboard and everything to shop for just when the shops have run out of their cheaper ranges and are pushing their more expensive ones!

MAKING PRESENTS

Sewing delights

You don't have to be super creative to make lovely personalized presents:

👍 Cushions are very easily and cheaply made, and sewing on a square of fabric from a much-loved (or children's outgrown) piece of clothing makes a very individual present

👍 For the talented, patchwork cushions from remnants of fabric can look superb

👍 Scarves are also very easy to make and can look stunning with interesting fabrics or sewn-on tassels, e.g. see **ehow.com**

Lots of websites can help you with designs, e.g. **makeitandmendit.com** *or* **makingyourown.co.uk**.

Soap and candles

It's easy to make a range of different flavoured and decorated soaps and candles. Visit **candleandsoap.about. com**, **soap-making-essentials.com** or **teachsoap.com**, which all have advice on how to make your soapy creations look professional.

The gift of handmade chocolate

It is surprisingly simple to make your own delicious truffles, which you can flavour with a tiny drop of rum or whisky if you like, and then coat in cocoa powder for that professional handmade look.

Store them in an airtight container in the fridge (for up to a week) and then when you are ready to give as a present, dust with a little extra cocoa powder and put in an old chocolate box that you have kept by precisely for this purpose.

There are thousands of recipes for truffles – many of them calling for specialist 'couverture' chocolate or for extensive use of blenders and fridges. My favourite, for ease of making and yumminess of taste, is the Waitrose recipe – go to **waitrose.com** *and enter 'plain chocolate truffles' in the search box and then select the recipes tab.*

Making liqueurs

Save attractive-looking small bottles through the year to put home-made drinks in. To make liqueur, freeze some picked raspberries or sloes. Then buy cheap gin or vodka when on special offer and in the autumn make sloe or raspberry gin or vodka – it's extremely easy to do. Check out **sloe.biz** for recipe advice or google 'cottage small holder raspberry gin' to find the raspberry gin recipe on **cottagesmallholder.com**.

You should make these liqueurs in the early autumn as they need three months to mature. Then bottle them out in the small bottles in December. A ribbon around the top, and you have a gorgeous-looking and tasting present – we get a bottle of this from my mother every year and always look forward to it.

Making a hamper

A hamper from Fortnum and Mason's is something most of us can only wish for, but a homemade hamper stuffed with goodies is something that all of us can make, for very little. Find a strong cardboard box and wrap it. Line it with tissue paper and put inside some jam or marmalade, biscuits, cordials, and a few chocolates. Then tie up the sealed box with ribbon – this can make a stunning present for very little expenditure.

Encourage children to give as well as to receive

Children often don't have money to buy presents, but they can make fabulous gifts. They love to join in the chocolate making (can't think why) and sewing, and many love drawing. Even the most artistically challenged child can make a great autobiographical picture of their favourite things to send to relatives.

You just need a large piece of paper and a few spare photographs they can cut and stick on, perhaps a picture or two of their favourite activities and/or a picture of their favourite food, possibly from its packaging. Then photocopy the collage for a lovely personal present easily shipped to all elderly relatives.

Reward the hard-working children with a free personalized video message from Santa – see **portablenorthpole.tv**.

> *Top tip: enforce thank you cards! Making kids write thank you cards makes them less keen to receive hundreds of presents.*

TRY SOMETHING DIFFERENT

Give an experience

Christmas needn't be about things. One of my most wonderful Christmas presents ever was a poem written for me. You can give friends or family promissory notes for a joint visit to the theatre, an exhibition or a sporting occasion.

Oxfam and other charities enable you to give the gift of giving at Christmas: your present pays for school meals for children in a developing country, for example, or buys a household a goat. As someone said: those who don't have Christmas in their heart will never find it under a tree.

Invent new rituals

Try inventing new family rituals around Christmas that don't involve hundreds of presents and over-eating, such as using the money saved by not giving gifts to pay for a holiday instead, or taking advantage of the empty roads to go on a long bicycle ride. Helping out at a charity at Christmas is a good way of bringing home to everyone how lucky they are – check out Crisis at Christmas, **crisis.org.uk**.

THE TRIMMINGS

The perfect Christmas tree? All Christmas trees are perfect!

You can get very lifelike artificial Christmas trees, which will last year after year and save on the pine needles all over your living room. Most importantly, after your initial investment you'll save upwards of £40 per year by not buying yet another real tree. Buy your artificial tree just after Christmas (in the January sales) and save it for next year.

Or buy a real tree in a good-sized pot, again in January, and plant it in the garden ready to be dug up come Christmas. And then replant it in the garden for next year, and the next ...

Decorations

👍 Buy decorations and crackers in the January sales when they are half-price and save them for next Christmas

👍 Make your own decorations – especially rewarding to do with children. Make paper lanterns and hang them across the room. Paper chains can be easily made with strips of paper joined with a bit of sellotape

👍 Bring natural things into your home – pine cones can be sprinkled with glitter and ivy can be tied up with red bows

👍 Avoid garden centres – go foraging instead

👍 Make a wreath for the door with some coat-hanger wire, sprigs of ivy and leftover Christmas baubles, e.g. see **housetohome.co.uk** for ideas

It's easy to make lovely homemade tree decorations with card (such as a 3D tree or star), e.g. see **enchantedlearning.com**.

Wrapping

👍 Save wrapping paper through the year and re-use at Christmas (especially good for small items as you can cut and use an uncreased bit)

👍 Enliven saved tissue paper with ribbon or stickers

👍 Make gift tags from cut-up Christmas cards – cut a shape with pinking shears and punch a hole with a hole puncher

👍 Alternatively, cut a rectangle of matching wrapping paper, double it over and write the 'to' and 'from' bit on the plain side, then attach to the wrapped gift with sellotape

👍 Approach your local florist and ask if you can buy a roll of their paper – this can be very cheap.

Christmas food that doesn't burst the budget

See the Daily Bread: Where to Shop chapter (page 53) for ways of saving money on food buying. Your Christmas food doesn't have to be top of the range – it's meeting with friends and family that really counts.

👍 Check out several supermarkets before Christmas so you can take advantage of special offers in a variety of places

👍 Go to Majestic to get a good deal on drink, or watch out for promotions in your local supermarket and stock up in advance

👍 If you're catering for a lot of people, don't be afraid of asking people to bring something specific to the feast

👍 If you're catering for vegetarians at Christmas and you're not sure where to start, look at **goodtoknow.co.uk** and search for vegetarian Christmas – you'll find you spend less than you would for a carnivore Christmas

👍 Limit your options – you don't really need a Christmas cake *and* a chocolate log, for example, so just choose one

Don't leave out leftovers

Make a list of menus for the festive season and build leftovers into your plan. Leftover turkey can be made into a great curry or soup, and bubble and squeak made from leftover veg is often a favourite. Potatoes are usually the 'glue' that holds the bubble and squeak mixture together, but then any other leftover veg can be put in and the resulting concoction made into patties and fried up. For a bit more taste, add some cheese or pop a fried egg on top.

Entertainment

Go back to good old-fashioned (and free) ways of enjoying yourselves, such as playing charades, hunt the thimble (or modern equivalent), cards or board games:

👍 The new Cluedo is bang up to date with 'Jack Mustard with a baseball bat in the home cinema' so children will be happy to play it

👍 Buy a bunch of dice (six per person) and you can play the great game of Perudo without the need to buy the swanky box it comes in – check out the rules at **perudo.com/perudo-rules**

👍 Yahtzee is another fun dice game that all the family can play – see **yahtzee.org.uk**.

👍 Check out **enjoyagame.com** for more ideas

👍 Or you could find a free carol service to attend and sing along to

> *Invest in a battery-charging kit and some rechargeable batteries before Christmas, just in case children are given toys that need batteries and you find the cupboard is bare.*

SUMMARY

Plan for Christmas – make presents beforehand, from simple scarves to delicious truffles; buy food before the last-minute rush when all the cheaper items have gone; buy only what you need. Make decorations for the tree and home and invent new family rituals which don't involve over-eating and mass indulgence. Don't make Christmas be about shopping and consumption – instead create an experience for your Christmas around charity, love, friends and family.

24. Know Your Rights

STAND UP FOR YOURSELF

Shops have to sell things for the price they advertise or label them for

This applies even if they are wrongly priced and the barcode when scanned brings up a different price. I once bought a huge pack of bacon this way – the shop had wrongly advertised it as costing £2.50 but it scanned at £6.50. The shop initially refused to let me buy it for the clearly labelled price, but later agreed to when I asked to speak to a manager and said, with a smile, that by Trading Standards rules they were obliged to sell it to me for the labelled price.

Check out what you are entitled to at **consumerdirect.gov.uk.**

Refunds

Shops are obliged to give refunds on all goods that are faulty, not fit for normal purpose or not as described. By Trading Standards rules, the following signs on goods or on adverts or marketing for goods are all illegal:

👍 No cash refunds

👍 No refunds or exchanges on sales goods

👍 Sold as seen

👍 No refunds or exchanges without a receipt

Repairs and replacements

If a product goes wrong, even after some months of use, then it's not fit for purpose and you're entitled to a repair, which should be carried out within a 'reasonable time' (there may be debate about what length of time is reasonable), or a replacement. You need proof of purchase, but this can be a bank or credit card statement and does not have to be a till receipt. You are entitled to a return of second goods, if you discover another defect other than the one shown to you when you bought it. Check out **whatconsumer.co.uk** for more help.

Speak up when things go wrong

If you suffer in silence, they have no incentive to improve or to prevent what went wrong for you going wrong for someone else.

Whether you didn't like your steak or you've been wrongly charged hundreds of pounds of bank charges, always *speak up when things go wrong as this gives the business a chance to put them right for you.*

How to write a complaint letter

I know many people who complain about service or price issues, but they don't get satisfaction. They end up just feeling unlucky or ignored. But often the problem is in the complaint letter they write – lack of clarity in the problem, or what you want done about it can easily lead to you not getting redress, even if the business in question has good intentions towards you. Any complaint letter is like a story – it needs a beginning, a middle, and an end.

1. **REPORT WHAT HAPPENED**
   State clearly and unemotionally what happened. Be specific with dates and times and names of any individuals you spoke to. Be clear about what the consequences have been for you – e.g. charges that have been made or losses that you have suffered.

2. **ASK FOR WHAT YOU WANT**
   State what you want to happen now – i.e. ask for a specific amount of money back, or for correct fitting of the product by a certain date etc. Be sure to show how you have arrived at figures, i.e. add the numbers up to show how you got to a total.

3. **THREATEN WHAT WILL HAPPEN IF THEY DON'T GIVE YOU WANT YOU WANT**
   In gently worded language, add a polite threat at the end, e.g. if they don't give you satisfaction, i.e. by reimbursing you what you request etc., you will take the matter further. So to any financial institution, say that you will take it to the financial ombudsman (free for you to contact), and to any business or individual, you can say that you will forward the letter to your MP if you don't have a favourable reply.

Always ask

Always ask for a raise from your boss, assuming you deserve it; always ask for a reduction in the price and try to find a reason for someone to give you a discount; always ask for the table in the window of the restaurant rather than just accepting the one by the toilets; always ask with a smile. If you don't ask, people won't necessarily give.

Always give

Always give back when you can – always check the gift aid box so that the government can contribute too; give your time in return for free food in a community allotment or a garden share scheme; always give something away if you can, rather than throwing it away.

Expect more and you may get it. If you do, you can return it too.

Index